WILLIAMS-SONOMA

ITALIAN

RECIPES AND TEXT
PAMELA SHELDON JOHNS

GENERAL EDITOR
CHUCK WILLIAMS

PHOTOGRAPHS
NOEL BARNHURST

SIMON & SCHUSTER • SOURCE

NEW YORK • LONDON • TORONTO • SYDNEY • SINGAPORE

CONTENTS

MAIN COURSES

VEGETABLES

DESSERTS

INTRODUCTION

During my many trips to Italy over the past forty years, I have always appreciated two qualities in Italian cooking: its simplicity and its vibrant, satisfying flavors. Whether served at home or in a restaurant, most meals are simple enough to prepare just before they are presented. Every course is enhanced by the use of fresh ingredients and natural flavorings. Olive oil, garlic, and aromatic herbs season pasta sauces, salads, meat, and fish. Citrus zest and nuts infuse such home-style desserts as gelato and biscotti. You will find all these offerings throughout this collection of Italian recipes.

If you have never prepared your own pasta dough, you will want to review the basics section at the back of the book. This section also covers making risotto, one of Italy's many signature dishes. Look for additional techniques and information in the glossary and in illustrated side notes accompanying all the recipes. With beautiful full-color photographs as inspiration, you will want to make these delicious Italian dishes part of your everyday cooking.

Chuck Williams

THE CLASSICS

Italy is composed of twenty geographically and culturally diverse regions, each with its own deeply rooted culinary specialties. Yet many of these local dishes, from the linguine with pesto of Liguria and the pizza Margherita of Campania to the osso buco of Lombardy, have crossed their regional borders to become national—and international—classics.

PIZZA MARGHERITA

To make the dough, in the bowl of a stand mixer, sprinkle the dry yeast over the warm water and let stand until foamy, about 4 minutes. If using fresh yeast, stir into the lukewarm water until dissolved. Place the bowl on the mixer fitted with the dough hook and add the olive oil, semolina flour, and salt; mix until combined. Add the all-purpose flour, ½ cup (2½ oz/75 g) at a time, and knead with the dough hook until the dough is smooth but not sticky, about 10 minutes.

Form the dough into a ball, put in a lightly oiled bowl, and turn to coat with oil. Cover the bowl with a kitchen towel and let rise in a warm, draft-free place until doubled in bulk, about 1 hour.

Preheat the oven to 450°F (230°C). If desired, place 2 pizza stones on the middle rack of the oven. Punch down the dough, transfer to a lightly floured work surface, and divide equally into 6 balls, kneading the balls briefly as you shape them. Cover with the towel and let rise until doubled in bulk, about 45 minutes.

Working with 2 balls of dough at a time, flatten each ball and gently stretch or roll into a round about 8 inches (20 cm) in diameter. Place the rounds on a flour-dusted baking sheet or pizza peel. Spread 2–3 tablespoons chopped tomatoes evenly over each round, leaving a ½-inch (12-mm) border around the edge of the dough. Distribute 3 or 4 mozzarella slices over the tomatoes. Sprinkle with salt to taste and drizzle with olive oil.

Place the pizzas in the oven or onto the preheated stones, if using. Bake until the edges are golden brown, 7–10 minutes. Using a spatula, remove the pizzas from the oven. Top each pizza with basil leaves. As each pair of pizzas bakes, assemble the next pizzas on a second baking sheet or on the pizza peel.

MAKES 6 SERVINGS

BUFFALO MOZZARELLA
Naples is considered the birthplace of pizza. The two traditional Neapolitan pizzas are the simple tomato-and-herb marinara and the Margherita, which is topped with tomatoes, *mozzarella di bufala,* and basil. The best mozzarella is made fresh from the milk of water buffalo. If you are unable to find it, substitute the cow's milk version, *fior di latte.* Both cheeses are soft, porcelain white, and quick melting. They come packed in whey for freshness and in several forms and sizes, from little mouthfuls called *bocconcini* or *cardinalini* to large rounds.

FOR THE DOUGH:

1 envelope (2½ teaspoons) active dry yeast or 1 cake compressed fresh yeast

1½ cups (12 fl oz/375 ml) warm water (105°–115°F/40°–46°C) for dry yeast or lukewarm water (80°–90°F/27°–32°C) for fresh yeast

2 tablespoons extra-virgin olive oil

½ cup (2½ oz/75 g) semolina flour

1 tablespoon salt

3–4 cups (15–20 oz/470–625 g) unbleached all-purpose (plain) flour, plus extra for dusting

6 fresh plum (Roma) tomatoes, coarsely chopped, or 6 canned whole tomatoes, preferably San Marzano, drained and coarsely chopped

¾ lb (375 g) buffalo mozzarella cheese, drained and cut into slices ¼ inch (6 mm) thick

Salt

Extra-virgin olive oil for drizzling

Fresh basil leaves for garnish

PASTA E FAGIOLI SOUP

1 cup (7 oz/220 g) dried cranberry or borlotti beans

2 cloves garlic

7 fresh rosemary sprigs

3 tablespoons extra-virgin olive oil

1 yellow onion, finely chopped

1 carrot, peeled and finely chopped

1 celery stalk, finely chopped

8 cups (64 fl oz/2 l) chicken stock (page 111)

1 tablespoon minced fresh flat-leaf (Italian) parsley

6 oz (185 g) fusilli or other dried shaped pasta

Salt and freshly ground pepper

Soak the dried beans in water to cover with the garlic and 1 of the rosemary sprigs *(right)*. Drain the beans, reserving the garlic and rosemary.

In a large saucepan over medium heat, heat the olive oil. Add the onion, carrot, and celery and sauté until the onion is golden, 6–8 minutes.

Add the chicken stock, drained beans, and reserved garlic and rosemary. Bring to a boil, reduce the heat to low, add the parsley, cover partially, and let simmer, stirring occasionally, until the beans are tender, 1–1½ hours. Raise the heat to medium, add the pasta, and cook until al dente, 8–10 minutes.

Remove and discard the rosemary sprig. Season the soup to taste with salt and pepper. Ladle into 6 warmed wide bowls, garnish with the remaining rosemary sprigs, and serve.

MAKES 6 SERVINGS

SOAKING BEANS

Dried beans *(fagioli)* need to be reconstituted before using in recipes. Pick over the beans and discard any misshapen beans or grit. Rinse the beans, put in a bowl, add water to cover generously and any herbs or other seasonings called for in a recipe, and let soak for at least 4 hours or up to overnight. Drain and use as directed. For a quick soak, combine the beans, water, and seasonings in a saucepan, bring to a rapid simmer, and simmer for 2 minutes, then cover and let stand off the heat for at least 1 hour. Drain well and use as directed.

LINGUINE WITH PESTO, GREEN BEANS, AND POTATOES

Bring a saucepan three-fourths full of water to a boil. Add the green beans and cook until tender-crisp, about 4 minutes. Using a slotted spoon, transfer the beans to a colander, rinse under running cold water, and drain. Return the water to a boil, add the potato slices, and cook until tender but firm, about 4 minutes. Drain, rinse under running cold water, and drain well.

Meanwhile, bring a large pot of water to a boil. Generously salt the boiling water, add the pasta, and cook the pasta until al dente, 7–8 minutes. Add the green beans and potatoes during the last minute of cooking. Drain, reserving 1 cup (8 fl oz/250 ml) of the pasta water.

Transfer the pasta, green beans, and potatoes to a warmed large, shallow bowl. Add the pesto and enough of the reserved pasta water to make a fluid sauce, and gently toss. Serve at once.

MAKES 6 SERVINGS

PESTO

To make this rich, bright green sauce from Liguria, process 3 cloves garlic in a food processor until coarsely chopped. Add 2 cups (2 oz/60 g) loosely packed fresh basil leaves and ¼ cup (1 oz/30 g) pine nuts, toasted (page 63), and process until finely chopped. With the machine running, gradually add ½ cup (4 fl oz/ 125 ml) extra-virgin olive oil. Transfer the pesto to a bowl and fold in ¼ cup (1 oz/30 g) freshly grated Parmesan cheese. Makes about 1 cup (8 fl oz/250 ml).

½ lb (250 g) green beans, trimmed and cut into 3-inch (7.5-cm) lengths

2 russet potatoes, peeled and cut into slices ½ inch (12 mm) thick

Salt

1 lb (500 g) dried linguine

Pesto *(far left)*

RISOTTO WITH MUSHROOMS

8–9 cups (64–72 fl oz/
2–2.25 l) chicken stock
(page 111)

½ cup (½ oz/15 g) dried
porcino mushrooms

¼ cup (2 fl oz/60 ml)
extra-virgin olive oil

4 cloves garlic, minced

½ lb (250 g) assorted
fresh wild mushrooms
such as shiitake, portobello,
oyster, and chanterelle,
stems removed and
caps brushed clean and
thinly sliced

½ lb (250 g) fresh white
mushrooms, stems
removed and caps brushed
clean and thinly sliced

¼ cup (⅓ oz/10 g)
minced fresh flat-leaf
(Italian) parsley

2 teaspoons minced
fresh thyme

3 cups (21 oz/655 g)
Arborio or Carnaroli rice

1 cup (8 fl oz/250 ml) dry
white wine, at room
temperature

2 tablespoons unsalted
butter

Salt and freshly ground
pepper

In a saucepan, bring the stock to a simmer. Remove from the heat and add the dried porcini. Let soak for 20 minutes. Drain the mushrooms through a sieve lined with a double layer of cheese-cloth (muslin), gently pressing against the mushrooms to force out the stock and reserving the stock. Return the stock to the saucepan and bring to a simmer over medium heat. Maintain at a gentle simmer over low heat. Chop the porcini and set aside.

In a large, heavy saucepan over medium heat, heat the olive oil. Add the garlic and sauté until softened, about 2 minutes. Add all of the fresh mushrooms and cook, stirring frequently, until softened, about 5 minutes. Add the chopped porcini, parsley, thyme, and ½ cup (4 fl oz/125 ml) of the simmering stock and cook until thickened, about 5 minutes. Using a slotted spoon, transfer the mushrooms to a bowl and set aside.

Add the rice to the same pan. Stir over medium heat until each grain is translucent with a white dot in the center, about 3 minutes. Add the wine and stir until completely absorbed.

Add the simmering stock a ladleful at a time, stirring frequently after each addition. Wait until the stock is almost completely absorbed (but the rice is never dry on top) before adding the next ladleful. Reserve ¼ cup (2 fl oz/60 ml) stock to add at the end.

When the rice is almost tender to the bite but slightly firm in the center and looks creamy, after about 18 minutes, add the mush-room mixture and a ladleful of stock. Cook, stirring occasionally, until the mushrooms are heated through and the rice is al dente, 2–3 minutes longer. Remove from the heat and stir in the butter and reserved ¼ cup stock. Season to taste with salt and pepper and serve at once.

MAKES 6 SERVINGS

PORCINO MUSHROOMS

Porcini (Italian for "little pigs")
are plump mushrooms with a
firm texture and full, earthy
flavor. Their large, smooth,
pale brown caps look similar
to cremini, but their stems
are thick and bulbous. These
woodland mushrooms grow in
the spring and autumn, when
the weather is warm and
damp, and are often found in
the vicinity of chestnut trees.
Fresh porcini are difficult to
find outside Europe; fortunately,
they are among the world's
best drying mushrooms. Dried
sliced porcini are packed with
flavor, and only a small amount
is needed to impart their
woodsy essence.

RIBOLLITA

RIBOLLITA

The ingredient that makes *ribollita* authentic is *cavolo nero*, "black cabbage," a dark green, leafy vegetable. (Dinosaur kale, a similar variety with deep green leaves, may be substituted.) *Ribollita* is a traditional Tuscan dish typically made over two or three days. It starts as a hearty vegetable soup. The soup is then layered, at the time of making or as leftovers the next day, with day-old bread to make *zuppa di pane,* or bread soup. When the soup is "reboiled" or baked until hot and drizzled with olive oil, it is declared *ribollita*. The version here is prepared and served the same day.

If using dried beans, place the soaked beans in a saucepan and add water to cover generously. Bring to a boil over high heat, reduce the heat to low, cover partially, and simmer until tender, 1–1½ hours. Drain the beans well. If using canned beans, drain well and set aside.

Chop the onion and celery stalk. Peel and chop the carrots and peel and dice the potato. Trim and dice the zucchini. In a large soup pot over medium-high heat, heat the ½ cup olive oil. Add the onion, celery, and carrots and sauté until the onion is golden, 3–4 minutes. Add the cauliflower and cook, stirring frequently, until tender-crisp, about 5 minutes. Add the *cavolo nero*, chard, zucchini, and potato (in that order) and cook, stirring, for 5 minutes.

Add the mixed herbs and the cooked dried or drained canned beans to the pot. Pour in the stock, bring to a boil over medium-high heat, and cook uncovered until the vegetables are tender, about 30 minutes. Season to taste with salt and pepper. Remove from the heat.

Meanwhile, preheat the oven to 425°F (220°C).

Ladle enough soup into a 9-by-13-inch (23-by-33-cm) baking dish to cover the bottom. Top with 4 or 5 bread slices, trimming them to fit if necessary, and then with a layer of soup. Sprinkle evenly with one-third of the Parmesan. Repeat the layers of bread, soup, and Parmesan two more times. Bake until heated through, about 20 minutes. Remove from the oven and drizzle with olive oil.

Ladle the *ribollita* into warmed soup bowls and serve.

MAKES 6 SERVINGS

1 cup (7 oz/220 g) dried cannellini beans, soaked (page 13), or 1 can (15 oz/470 g) cannellini beans

1 yellow onion

1 celery stalk

2 carrots

1 large boiling potato

2 zucchini (courgettes)

½ cup (4 fl oz/125 ml) extra-virgin olive oil, plus extra for drizzling

1 cup (3 oz/90 g) coarsely chopped cauliflower florets

4 or 5 *cavolo nero* leaves *(far left)* or dinosaur kale leaves, shredded

1 cup (2 oz/60 g) shredded Swiss chard leaves

¼ cup (⅓ oz/10 g) minced fresh herbs, including fresh flat-leaf (Italian) parsley, rosemary, and sage

2½ qt (2.5 l) chicken or vegetable stock (page 111)

Salt and freshly ground pepper

12–15 slices day-old coarse country bread, with crusts

½ cup (2 oz/60 g) freshly grated Parmesan cheese

BISTECCA ALLA FIORENTINA

2 cups (14 oz/440 g) dried
cannellini beans, soaked
(page 13), or 2 cans (15 oz/
470 g each) cannellini
beans

3 tablespoons extra-virgin
olive oil, plus extra for
brushing

Salt and freshly ground
pepper

2 T-bone or porterhouse
steaks, 3½–4 lb (1.75–2 kg)
total weight and
1½–2 inches (4–5 cm)
thick

1 tablespoon minced
fresh thyme

1 bunch arugula, stemmed

2 lemons, quartered

If using dried beans, place the soaked beans in a large saucepan and add water to cover generously. Bring to a boil over high heat, reduce the heat to low, cover partially, and simmer until tender, 1–1½ hours. Drain the beans well. Return to the pan, stir in the 3 tablespoons olive oil, season to taste with salt and pepper, and keep warm. If using canned beans, drain them well, place in a large saucepan over low heat, stir in the 3 tablespoons olive oil, and season to taste with salt and pepper. Cook the beans until heated through, then remove from the heat and keep warm.

Meanwhile, prepare a charcoal fire in an outdoor grill and let burn until the coals are covered with white ash. Leave the coals heaped in the center of the grill; do not spread them out. For a gas grill, preheat on high heat. Brush the grill rack with oil.

Sprinkle the steaks with salt and pepper. Using tongs (to avoid piercing the meat), set the steaks on the rack and grill, turning once, until the meat is brown and seared on the outside and cooked rare in the center, 15–18 minutes total, or until done to taste *(right)*. To make crosshatch grill marks, rotate the meat 90 degrees once while cooking on the first side.

Transfer the beans to a serving bowl and sprinkle with the thyme. Arrange a bed of arugula on a platter. Place the steaks on top, sprinkle with pepper, and accompany with the lemon quarters. To serve, cut the steaks into thick slices and offer the beans alongside.

Note: This famed Florentine dish traditionally uses the Chianina beef of Tuscany. In its place, seek out high-quality beef or free-range beef. Here, the steaks are served with another Tuscan staple, cannellini beans.

MAKES 4 SERVINGS

GRILLING BEEF

Different temperature zones of the grill can be used to cook steaks to the desired doneness. Grill steaks 2 inches (5 cm) thick over the hottest part of the fire, turning them once and moving them to the perimeter of the grill if flare-ups occur, 15–18 minutes total for rare, 18–22 minutes for medium. For well-done steaks, grill them over high heat for 18–25 minutes, then move to a cooler part of the grill and cook for 5–10 minutes. An instant-read thermometer should register 120°–125°F (49°–52°C) for rare, 140°F (60 °C) for medium, and 150°–160°F (65°–71°C) for well done.

PAPPARDELLE WITH RAGÙ ALLA BOLOGNESE

In a large saucepan over medium-high heat, heat the olive oil. Add the pancetta, onion, celery, and carrot and sauté until the onion is golden, 4–5 minutes.

Add the beef and pork and sauté over medium-high heat until lightly browned, 3–4 minutes. Add the stock, bring to a boil, reduce the heat to low, and simmer, stirring frequently, until thickened, 35–40 minutes. Stir in the tomato paste and heat through. Season to taste with salt and pepper.

Meanwhile, bring a large pot of water to a boil. Generously salt the boiling water, add the pasta, and cook until al dente, 2–3 minutes. Drain and transfer to a warmed large, shallow bowl. Spoon the sauce over the pasta and serve at once.

Note: Ask your butcher to chop the beef and pork for you. Or, purchase the meats coarsely ground (minced).

MAKES 6 SERVINGS

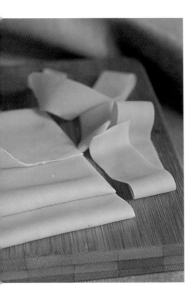

PAPPARDELLE

These wide ribbons of pasta, ranging from ½ inch (12 mm) to 1 inch (2.5 cm) in width, are ideal for serving with hearty sauces like Bolognese meat sauce. After rolling out the pasta dough (page 110) and letting it rest, lay the sheet on a lightly floured work surface. Using a straight-edged pastry wheel or a sharp, thin-bladed knife, cut the pasta for this dish into ribbons 1 inch wide. Dried pappardelle, sold in well-stocked grocery stores or specialty-food stores, may be used in place of fresh pasta; increase the cooking time to 7–8 minutes.

¼ cup (2 fl oz/60 ml) extra-virgin olive oil

¼ lb (125 g) pancetta (page 51), finely chopped

1 yellow onion, finely chopped

1 celery stalk, finely chopped

1 carrot, peeled and finely chopped

½ lb (250 g) beef shoulder or rump, finely chopped (see Note)

¼ lb (125 g) pork, finely chopped (see Note)

1½ cups (12 fl oz/375 ml) meat stock (page 111)

3 tablespoons tomato paste

Salt and freshly ground pepper

Fresh pasta dough (page 110), cut into ribbons 1 inch (2.5 cm) wide *(far left)*

OSSO BUCO WITH RISOTTO ALLA MILANESE

¾ cup (4 oz/125 g) unbleached all-purpose (plain) flour

Salt and freshly ground pepper

6 veal shanks, about 6 lb 3 kg) total weight, cut crosswise 1 inch (2.5 cm) thick

¾ cup (6 fl oz/180 ml) extra-virgin olive oil

1 yellow onion, coarsely chopped, plus ½ cup (2½ oz/75 g) finely chopped

1 carrot, peeled and diced

1 celery stalk, diced

2 cloves garlic, minced

1½ cups (12 fl oz/375 ml) dry red wine

11 cups (88 fl oz/2.75 l) meat stock (page 111)

3 cups (21 oz/655 g) Arborio or Carnaroli rice

1 cup (8 fl oz/250 ml) dry white wine

2 pinches of saffron threads soaked in ¼ cup (2 fl oz/ 60 ml) warm meat stock

¼ cup (2 oz/60 g) unsalted butter

1 cup (4 oz/125 g) freshly grated Parmesan cheese

Gremolata *(far right)*

Put the flour in a wide, shallow bowl and season with salt and pepper. Dredge the veal shanks, coating them evenly and shaking off the excess. In a large, heavy frying pan over medium-high heat, heat ½ cup (4 fl oz/120 ml) of the olive oil. Add the veal and brown for about 4 minutes on each side. Transfer to a plate.

Return the pan to medium heat, add the coarsely chopped onion, carrot, celery, and garlic, and sauté until softened, 3–4 minutes. Add the red wine and deglaze the pan, stirring to scrape up the browned bits from the pan bottom. Raise the heat to high and cook until the liquid is thickened and reduced by half, 3–4 minutes. Add 5 cups (40 fl oz/1.25 l) of the stock and bring to a boil. Reduce the heat to low, return the veal to the pan, cover, and simmer, turning occasionally, for 1 hour. Uncover and cook until the veal is tender, about 30 minutes longer.

Meanwhile, in a saucepan over medium heat, bring the remaining 6 cups (48 fl oz/1.5 l) stock to a gentle simmer and maintain over low heat. In a large, heavy saucepan over medium heat, warm the remaining ¼ cup (2 fl oz/60 ml) oil. Add the finely chopped onion and sauté until softened, 4–5 minutes. Add the rice and stir until each grain is translucent with a white dot in the center, 3–4 minutes. Add the white wine and stir until completely absorbed.

Add the simmering stock a ladleful at a time, stirring frequently after each addition. Wait until the stock is almost completely absorbed (but the rice is never dry on top) before adding the next ladleful. Reserve about ¼ cup (2 fl oz/60 ml) stock to add at the end. When the rice is tender to the bite but slightly firm in the center and looks creamy, after about 18 minutes, add the saffron mixture. Stir in the butter, cheese, and reserved stock. Season with salt and pepper. Transfer the risotto to a warmed platter. Top with the veal shanks, sprinkle with the *gremolata,* and serve at once.

MAKES 6 SERVINGS

GREMOLATA

A traditional garnish for osso buco, *gremolata* is sprinkled over the veal shanks at the end of cooking or is offered at the table to season individual portions of the finished dish. The heat releases the oils from the *gremolata,* distributing its fresh flavor. To make the *gremolata,* combine ½ cup (¾ oz/20 g) minced fresh flat-leaf (Italian) parsley, the finely grated zest of 1 lemon, and 2 cloves garlic, minced, in a small bowl and stir to blend. *Gremolata* also complements other veal dishes such as pasta with veal sauce, or vegetables such as green beans. Makes about ½ cup (¾ oz/20 g).

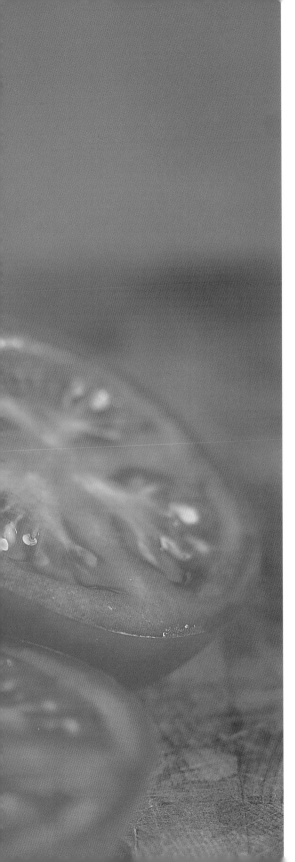

ANTIPASTI

An Italian meal typically begins with an antipasto, a small dish—or sometimes two or three dishes—designed to stimulate the appetite for what is to follow. It might be as simple as the tomato-and-bread salad known as panzanella *or as complex as the tender deep-fried seafood and vegetables in* fritto misto.

TRIO OF CROSTINI
28

CIPOLLINE IN AGRODOLCE
31

INSALATA FRUTTI DI MARE
32

PANZANELLA
35

FRITTO MISTO
36

FRITTATA WITH SWEET PEPPERS AND SAUSAGE
39

VITELLO TONNATO
40

TRIO OF CROSTINI

In a sauté pan over medium heat, heat 2 tablespoons of the olive oil. Add the yellow onion, carrot, and celery and sauté until the onion is golden, 3–4 minutes. Add the beans, ½ cup (4 fl oz/125 ml) of the stock, the garlic, and the rosemary. Simmer, uncovered, until most of the stock has evaporated, about 10 minutes. Remove from the heat, season to taste with salt and pepper, and let cool to room temperature.

Melt the butter with the remaining 2 tablespoons oil in a sauté pan over medium heat. Add the pancetta and white onion, and sauté until the onion is golden, 3–4 minutes. Add the chicken livers and remaining ½ cup stock, and cook until the livers are firm to the touch and the stock has thickened, 12–15 minutes. Add the wine and stir to scrape up the browned bits from the pan bottom. Remove from the heat and let cool to room temperature.

In a food processor, purée the bean mixture until smooth. Transfer the bean purée to a bowl and wash the processor work bowl. Purée the liver mixture until smooth. Transfer the liver purée to a bowl, stir in the minced parsley and thyme, and season to taste with salt and pepper.

Spread a thin layer of the bean purée onto 6 *crostini* and garnish each with a tomato slice. Repeat with the liver purée, topping the *crostini* with the apple slices, and then with the olive spread, topping the *crostini* with the parsley leaves. Serve at once.

MAKES 6 SERVINGS

OLIVE SPREAD

In Italy, some olive varieties are made into olive oil; others are used in pasta sauces, meat and fish dishes, and spreads like this one for *crostini*. Mature black olives, whose full flavor is preferred in cooking, are cured in salt, oil, or brine and are sometimes marinated with herbs and spices. To make the olive spread, combine 1 cup (6 oz/185 g) oil- or brine-cured black olives, pitted; 2 table-spoons extra-virgin olive oil; and ½ teaspoon finely grated orange zest in a food processor and pulse until smooth.

4 tablespoons (2 fl oz/60 ml) extra-virgin olive oil

2 tablespoons *each* finely chopped yellow onion, carrot, and celery

¾ cup (5 oz/155 g) drained canned cannellini beans

1 cup (8 fl oz/250 ml) chicken stock (page 111)

1 clove garlic, minced

½ teaspoon minced fresh rosemary

Salt and freshly ground pepper

1 tablespoon unsalted butter

2 tablespoons finely chopped pancetta (page 51)

½ white onion, finely chopped

6 oz (185 g) chicken livers

¼ cup (2 fl oz/60 ml) dry white wine

1 tablespoon minced fresh flat-leaf (Italian) parsley, plus 6 leaves

½ teaspoon minced fresh thyme

18 *crostini* (page 110)

6 thin slices *each* oil-packed sun-dried tomato and Red Delicious apple

Olive spread *(far left)*

CIPOLLINE IN AGRODOLCE

2 cups (16 fl oz/500 ml) white wine vinegar

2 cups (16 fl oz/500 ml) balsamic vinegar (see Notes)

3 tablespoons granulated sugar

3 tablespoons firmly packed brown sugar

¼ teaspoon salt

1 lb (500 g) *cipolline* onions (see Notes), about 1½ inches (4 cm) in diameter

In a nonaluminum saucepan, combine the white wine and balsamic vinegars, granulated and brown sugars, and salt. Bring to a boil over medium-high heat, stirring to dissolve the sugars. Add the onions and cook until softened when pierced with the tip of a knife, 2–3 minutes. Let cool for about 1 hour.

Transfer the onions and liquid to a nonaluminum container, making sure that the onions remain submerged in the liquid. Cover and let stand for 1 week at room temperature before using, to allow the onions to mellow and absorb the flavors. The onions will keep for up to 6 months in the refrigerator.

Notes: For this recipe, an inexpensive, young balsamic vinegar may be used in place of a more expensive aged vinegar. Cipolline onions are small, flat Italian onions, usually 1–3 inches (2.5–7.5 cm) in diameter. They are available in some supermarkets and farmers' markets. Pearl onions or small boiling onions may be substituted.

Serving Tip: Using a slotted spoon, transfer the onions to a small dish and offer alongside a platter of cheese and sliced meats, such as prosciutto (page 64).

MAKES 6–8 SERVINGS

AGRODOLCE

Meaning "sweet and sour," *agrodolce* is an ancient preparation that was used to preserve foods before the days of refrigeration. Today, the combination of sweet and tart flavors is found in condiments (balsamic vinegar is the definitive example), marinades, and sauces. Vinegar and sugar are the two basic elements of *agrodolce*. Myriad variations may employ wine or citrus juice or zest for the sour flavor; raisins are a frequent source of the sweet. Meat, fish, and vegetables, particularly onions, are excellent cooked in *agrodolce*.

INSALATA FRUTTI DI MARE

Bring a saucepan three-fourths full of water to a boil. Add the shrimp and cook just until they turn bright pink, about 2 minutes. Drain, rinse under running cold water, drain again, and set aside. Cut the squid bodies into rings about ½ inch (12 mm) wide. Leave the tentacles whole. Set aside.

In a large sauté pan over medium-high heat, heat ¼ cup (2 fl oz/ 60 ml) of the olive oil. Add the onion and sauté until softened but not browned, 2–3 minutes. Add the scallops and cook until tender, 3–5 minutes. Add the wine and squid and continue to cook until the squid is opaque and the wine is almost evaporated, 2–3 minutes longer. Add the shrimp, remove from the heat, and let cool to room temperature.

Transfer the seafood to a large bowl. Add the olives, capers, parsley, garlic, lemon juice, and remaining ¼ cup olive oil. Season to taste with salt and pepper and toss well. Serve at room temperature or chilled.

To serve, place a lettuce leaf on each individual plate and top with the salad, dividing it evenly.

MAKES 6 SERVINGS

¼ lb (125 g) shrimp (prawns), peeled and deveined (page 115)

½ lb (250 g) cleaned squid (page 115)

½ cup (4 fl oz/120 ml) extra-virgin olive oil

¼ cup (1 oz/30 g) finely chopped yellow onion

¼ lb (125 g) bay scallops

¼ cup (2 fl oz/60 ml) dry white wine

½ cup (2½ oz/75 g) oil-cured black olives, pitted and coarsely chopped

2 tablespoons salt-cured capers, rinsed and drained

1 tablespoon minced fresh flat-leaf (Italian) parsley

2 cloves garlic, minced

Juice of 1 lemon

Salt and freshly ground pepper

6 red-leaf lettuce leaves

PANZANELLA

3 cups (6 oz/185 g) day-old Italian bread cubes (1 inch/2.5 cm)

2 large ripe tomatoes, seeded and diced

1 English (hothouse) cucumber, peeled, halved lengthwise, seeded, and diced

½ cup (2½ oz/75 g) finely chopped red onion

3 cloves garlic, minced

¼ cup (2 fl oz/60 ml) red wine vinegar

¾ cup (6 fl oz/180 ml) extra-virgin olive oil

Salt and freshly ground pepper

Fresh basil leaves for garnish

Preheat the oven to 400°F (200°C). Spread the bread cubes on a baking sheet. Place in the oven and bake, turning once or twice, until lightly toasted, about 5 minutes. Set aside and let cool.

Place the bread cubes in a large bowl, and add the tomatoes, cucumber, and red onion.

In a small bowl, combine the garlic and vinegar. Whisking constantly, gradually drizzle in the olive oil *(right)*. Whisk until well blended and season to taste with salt and pepper.

Pour the dressing over the salad and toss well. Garnish with the basil leaves and serve at once.

MAKES 6 SERVINGS

MAKING EMULSION DRESSINGS

An emulsion is a stabilized mixture of two or more liquids that would ordinarily not combine, such as oil and vinegar. Some emulsions are temporary, such as vinaigrette; others are more stable, like mayonnaise. Stable emulsions require an emulsifying agent such as mustard or egg yolks to help bind the ingredients. Both types of emulsions require vigorous blending. When making the vinaigrette for this Tuscan salad, slowly drizzle the oil into the other ingredients as you whisk to create a creamy, well-emulsified dressing.

FRITTO MISTO

Trim the zucchini. Cut each zucchini crosswise into slices ¼ inch (6 mm) thick. Cut the squid bodies crosswise into rings ¼ inch (6 mm) wide. Pat the squid rings, shrimp, and clams dry. Set aside.

To make the batter, in a bowl, combine the flour, ½ teaspoon salt, and ¼ teaspoon pepper. Add the milk, egg yolks, and olive oil. Stir to blend. In another bowl, using a handheld mixer on high speed or a balloon whisk, beat the egg whites until soft peaks form, about 2 minutes. Using a large rubber spatula, carefully fold the beaten whites into the milk mixture just until blended.

Preheat the oven to 200°F (95°C). Pour peanut oil to a depth of 1 inch (2.5 cm) into a large, heavy sauté pan and heat to 365°F (185°C) on a deep-frying thermometer. A drop of batter slipped into the oil should rise immediately to the surface.

Working in small batches to avoid overcrowding the pan, use tongs to dip the shrimp, squid, clams, zucchini slices, and mushrooms in the batter to coat evenly, letting the excess batter drip back into the bowl. Slip into the hot oil and fry, turning once, until golden brown, about 2 minutes on each side. Using clean tongs, remove each piece from the pan and place on a baking sheet lined with several layers of paper towels to drain. Transfer to a platter and keep warm in the oven while frying the remaining seafood and vegetables. Be sure to let the oil return to 365°F before frying each new batch *(left)*.

Sprinkle with the parsley, coarse salt, and pepper to taste. Serve with lemon wedges.

Caution: When deep-frying foods, do not heat the oil above 375°F (190°C). If it reaches 400°F (200°C) or more, it may start to smoke, then burst into flame.

MAKES 6 SERVINGS

2 zucchini (courgettes)

½ lb (250 g) cleaned squid bodies (page 115)

12 shrimp (prawns), peeled, with tail segment intact, and deveined (page 115)

1 lb (500 g) small hard-shelled clams such as manila or littleneck, shelled

1 cup (5 oz/155 g) unbleached all-purpose (plain) flour

Salt and freshly ground pepper

1 cup (8 fl oz/250 ml) whole milk

2 large eggs, separated

1 tablespoon extra-virgin olive oil

Peanut oil or canola oil for deep-frying

½ lb (250 g) small fresh white mushrooms, about 1 inch (2.5 cm) in diameter, stems removed and caps brushed clean

2 tablespoons minced fresh flat-leaf (Italian) parsley

Coarse salt for sprinkling

2 lemons, cut into wedges

FRITTATA WITH SWEET PEPPERS AND SAUSAGE

1 tablespoon minced fresh flat-leaf (Italian) parsley

6 large eggs, lightly beaten

Salt and freshly ground pepper

3 tablespoons extra-virgin olive oil

1 small yellow onion, cut into ¼-inch (6-mm) dice

1 lb (500 g) Italian sausages *(far right),* cut into slices ¼ inch (6 mm) thick

1 small red bell pepper (capsicum), seeded and cut into ¼-inch (6-mm) dice

1 small yellow bell pepper (capsicum), seeded and cut into ¼-inch (6-mm) dice

¼ cup (1 oz/30 g) freshly grated Parmesan cheese, plus extra for sprinkling

Preheat the oven to 425°F (220°C). In a bowl, stir the parsley into the eggs and season with salt and pepper. Set aside.

In a medium ovenproof frying pan over medium heat, heat the olive oil. Add the onion and sausages and sauté until lightly browned, about 5 minutes. Add the red and yellow bell peppers and cook until softened, 2–3 minutes. Distribute the vegetables and sausages evenly in the pan. Pour the egg mixture over the sausage mixture and cook, using a spatula to lift the edges as they firm up to allow the liquid egg to flow under, until the eggs are just beginning to set on the sides and bottom of the pan, 3–4 minutes.

Evenly sprinkle the ¼ cup Parmesan on top of the eggs, place the pan in the oven, and bake until a knife inserted in the center of the frittata comes out clean, 20–25 minutes. Serve the frittata hot or at room temperature, cut into wedges and sprinkled with Parmesan.

MAKES 6 SERVINGS

ITALIAN SAUSAGES

Most of the fresh sausages in Italy are made from pork, and many are flavored with a variety of seasonings, such as fennel seed, garlic, peppercorns, or dried red chiles. Each area of the country produces its own distinctive sausages, from the intensely hot, spicy sausages of Calabria in the south to the sweetly spiced products of Emilia-Romagna in the north. To complement the bell peppers in this frittata, use either spicy or sweet sausages. Look for Italian sausages in the meat department of well-stocked markets and in Italian delicatessens.

VITELLO TONNATO

One day ahead, place the cloves on a square of cheesecloth (muslin), gather the corners, and tie with kitchen string to make a bundle. Combine the wine, vinegar, and clove bundle in a large nonaluminum bowl. Add the veal, turn to coat in the marinade, cover, and refrigerate for at least 4 hours or up to overnight, turning the veal occasionally.

After the veal has marinated, remove and discard the cloves, and transfer the meat and marinade to a large pot. Add 2 cups (16 fl oz/ 500 ml) water, season with salt, and bring to a boil over medium-high heat. Reduce the heat to medium, cover, and cook until the veal is tender, about 1 hour. Remove from the heat and let cool for 1 hour in the cooking liquid.

To make the tuna sauce, combine the 2 tablespoons capers and the anchovies in a wooden chopping bowl, and chop with a *mezzaluna (left)* until a paste forms. Alternatively, combine the capers and anchovies on a cutting board and chop with a large chef's knife until a paste forms. Using a fork, flake the tuna into a bowl. Add the anchovy mixture, mayonnaise, and lemon zest. Blend gently until smooth. Season to taste with salt and pepper. Set aside.

Using a slotted spoon, remove the veal from the pot, allowing any excess liquid to drain back into the pot, and place on a cutting board. Cut the veal across the grain into slices ⅛ inch (3 mm) thick. Arrange the slices on a platter, overlapping them, and spread evenly with the tuna sauce. Sprinkle with the parsley, bell pepper, and 1 tablespoon capers. Refrigerate for at least 30 minutes or up to 3 hours before serving.

MAKES 6 SERVINGS

USING A MEZZALUNA

For preparing the tuna sauce for the veal in this recipe, a *mezzaluna* is an efficient tool. *Mezzaluna* means "half-moon," an apt name for this cutting tool with a crescent-shaped blade. It is held with both hands and used with a rhythmic rocking motion to chop foods uniformly, and more quickly, safely, and easily than with a chef's knife. It may be used on a cutting board or in a shallow wooden bowl. For this recipe, rock the *mezzaluna* blade over the capers and anchovies, without lifting it, until the ingredients are chopped to the consistency of a paste.

4 whole cloves

1 bottle (750 ml) dry white wine

1 cup (8 fl oz/250 ml) white wine vinegar

1 lb (500 g) boneless veal rump

Salt

FOR THE TUNA SAUCE:

2 tablespoons salt-cured capers (page 32), rinsed and drained

2 olive oil–packed anchovy fillets

1 cup (7 oz/220 g) drained olive oil–packed tuna

1 cup (8 oz/250 g) mayonnaise

1 teaspoon finely grated lemon zest

Salt and freshly ground pepper

1 tablespoon minced fresh flat-leaf (Italian) parsley

1 tablespoon finely diced red bell pepper (capsicum)

1 tablespoon salt-cured capers, rinsed and drained

PASTA

Italians distinguish between two types of pasta: pasta secca, *or "dry pasta," and* pasta fresca, *or "fresh pasta." The first, such as bucatini and spaghetti, is machine made, sold packaged, and traditionally a product of the south, while the second, such as ravioli and cannelloni, is usually rolled and shaped by hand, especially in homes of the north.*

ORECCHIETTE WITH BROCCOLI RABE AND CLAMS

Discard any clams that fail to close to the touch. Put the clams in a large pot with 1 inch (2.5 cm) of water. Cover, bring to a boil, and cook over high heat for 1 minute, shaking the pan occasionally. Using a slotted spoon, transfer the clams that have opened to a bowl; cook any remaining clams for a few seconds longer until they open. Transfer any remaining clams that have opened to the bowl and let cool to the touch. Discard any clams that failed to open. Reserve the cooking liquid.

Bring a large pot of water to a boil. Meanwhile, remove the clam meat from the shells, holding them over a bowl to catch the juices. Rinse the clams well to remove any sand and chop coarsely. Set aside. Strain the juices and cooking liquid through a sieve lined with cheesecloth (muslin) to remove any sand and set aside.

Generously salt the boiling water, add the pasta, and cook until al dente, about 8 minutes. Drain and set aside.

In a large sauté pan over medium-high heat, heat the olive oil. Add the onion and sauté until lightly golden, 2–3 minutes. Add the garlic, red pepper flakes to taste, and broccoli rabe and cook, stirring, for 1 minute. Add the tomatoes and reserved clams and clam cooking liquid and bring to a boil. Reduce the heat to low, add the orecchiette, and toss to coat with the sauce. Stir in the parsley and salt and black pepper to taste. Serve at once.

MAKES 6 SERVINGS

BROCCOLI RABE

Also known as broccoli raab, rape, and *rapini*, broccoli rabe paired with orecchiette is a traditional dish in Apulia and other regions. This bright green vegetable, with its slender stalks and small florets, resembles broccoli but has many more leaves, which are small and jagged. Related to cabbage and turnips, broccoli rabe has a mild, pleasantly bitter taste. Remove any tough stems and wilted leaves before cooking. If the skin on the lower part of the stalks seems fibrous, peel with a vegetable peeler.

36 small hard-shelled clams such as manila or littleneck, well scrubbed

Salt and freshly ground black pepper

1 lb (500 g) dried orecchiette

3 tablespoons extra-virgin olive oil

½ cup (2 oz/60 g) chopped yellow onion

4 cloves garlic, minced

Pinch of red pepper flakes, or to taste

½ lb (250 g) broccoli rabe, trimmed and cut into 3-inch (7.5-cm) pieces

3 ripe tomatoes, peeled and seeded (page 47), then coarsely chopped

1 tablespoon minced fresh flat-leaf (Italian) parsley

BUCATINI ALL'AMATRICIANA

½ cup (4 fl oz/125 ml)
extra-virgin olive oil

¼ lb (125 g) pancetta
(page 51), diced

1 yellow onion, diced

Pinch of red pepper flakes,
or to taste

4 ripe tomatoes, peeled
and seeded *(far right)*,
then chopped

Salt and freshly ground
black pepper

1 lb (500 g) bucatini or
spaghetti

Bring a large pot of water to a boil. Meanwhile, in a large sauté pan over medium-high heat, heat the olive oil. Add the pancetta, onion, and red pepper flakes to taste and cook until the onion is golden, 3–4 minutes. Add the tomatoes and cook until slightly thickened, 5–6 minutes. Season to taste with salt and black pepper.

Generously salt the boiling water, add the pasta, and cook until al dente, 8–10 minutes. Drain the pasta well, add it to the frying pan, and toss well with the sauce to heat through.

Pour the pasta and sauce into a warmed large, shallow bowl and serve at once.

MAKES 6 SERVINGS

PREPARING TOMATOES

Amatrice, a small town northeast of Rome, gave its name to this spicy tomato sauce traditionally served with spaghetti but here paired with bucatini. To peel and seed the tomatoes for the sauce, bring a saucepan of water to a boil. Using a sharp knife, score a shallow X in the blossom end of each tomato. Immerse the tomatoes in the boiling water and leave for 15–30 seconds, or until the skins just begin to wrinkle. Remove the tomatoes with a slotted spoon, let cool slightly, then peel away the skins. Cut in half crosswise and squeeze gently to dislodge the seeds.

MUSHROOM RAVIOLI WITH WALNUT SAUCE

In a small bowl, combine the dried porcini and heated stock. Soak for 20 minutes. Drain the mushrooms through a sieve lined with a double layer of cheesecloth (muslin), gently pressing against the mushrooms to force out the stock and reserving the stock. Chop the porcini and set aside. Trim the stems from the fresh mushrooms and discard. Coarsely chop the caps and set aside.

In a large sauté pan over medium heat, heat the 3 tablespoons olive oil. Add the minced garlic and sauté until softened, about 2 minutes. Add the fresh mushrooms and sauté until softened, about 5 minutes. Add the parsley, thyme, porcini, and reserved stock and cook, stirring occasionally, until the liquid has thickened, about 10 minutes. Let cool for 20–30 minutes. Transfer the mushroom mixture to a bowl. Add the ricotta and ¼ cup (1 oz/ 30 g) of the Parmesan and mix well. Season to taste with salt, white pepper, and nutmeg. Set aside.

To assemble the ravioli, roll out the pasta dough as directed on page 110, and then cut and fill *(left)*. Bring a large pot of water to a boil.

Meanwhile, combine the 2 cloves garlic, 1 cup (4 oz/125 g) of the walnuts, and the bread mixture in a food processor and pulse until smooth. With the machine running, drizzle in the ¼ cup olive oil and process to make a smooth sauce. Pour into a bowl, stir in the remaining ½ cup (2 oz/60 g) Parmesan, and season to taste with salt and white pepper.

Generously salt the boiling water, add the ravioli, and cook until al dente, about 3 minutes. Drain and place in a warmed large, shallow bowl. Add the walnut sauce and toss gently to coat the ravioli. Sprinkle with Parmesan and the remaining ¼ cup (1 oz/ 30 g) walnuts, and serve at once.

MAKES 8 SERVINGS

ASSEMBLING PASTA TRIANGLES

In a small bowl, beat together 1 egg with 1 teaspoon water. Lay the pasta sheets flat on a lightly floured work surface. Using a straight-edged pastry wheel or a sharp, thin-bladed knife, cut the dough into 5-inch (13-cm) squares. Spoon 1 tablespoon of the mushroom filling onto the center of each square. Lightly brush the edges with the egg wash. Fold the square in half on the diagonal to form a triangle. Using your fingers, press the edges to seal. Make sure that the filling does not break the seal, or the triangle will come apart when cooked.

½ cup (½ oz/15 g) dried porcino mushrooms

½ cup (4 fl oz/125 ml) chicken stock (page 111), heated

1 lb (500 g) assorted fresh mushrooms such as shiitake, portobello, oyster, and chanterelle, brushed clean

¼ cup (2 fl oz/60 ml) plus 3 tablespoons extra-virgin olive oil

4 cloves garlic, minced, plus 2 whole cloves

2 tablespoons minced fresh flat-leaf (Italian) parsley

2 teaspoons minced fresh thyme

½ cup (4 oz/125 g) whole-milk ricotta cheese

¾ cup (3 oz/90 g) freshly grated Parmesan cheese, plus extra for sprinkling

Salt, freshly ground white pepper, and freshly grated nutmeg

2 lb (1 kg) pasta dough (page 110)

1¼ cups (5 oz/155 g) walnuts, toasted (page 90) and coarsely chopped

2 slices coarse country bread soaked in 1 cup (8 fl oz/250 ml) milk

SPAGHETTI ALLA CARBONARA

2 tablespoons extra-virgin olive oil

1 yellow onion, finely diced

¼ lb (125 g) pancetta, finely diced

Salt and coarsely ground pepper

1 lb (500 g) spaghetti

4 large egg yolks, beaten

½ cup (4 fl oz/125 ml) heavy (double) cream

1 cup (4 oz/125 g) freshly grated Parmesan cheese

3 tablespoons minced fresh flat-leaf (Italian) parsley

Bring a large pot of water to a boil. Meanwhile, in a sauté pan over medium-high heat, heat the olive oil. Add the onion and sauté until softened but not browned, about 2 minutes. Add the pancetta and cook until lightly browned, 2–3 minutes. Remove from the heat and let cool slightly.

Generously salt the boiling water, add the pasta, and cook until al dente, 7–8 minutes. While the pasta is cooking, in a large bowl, whisk together the egg yolks, cream, and Parmesan. Add the pancetta mixture and season with salt. Set aside.

Drain the pasta well, add to the bowl, and toss with the egg mixture until well coated. Turn into a warmed large, shallow bowl, sprinkle with parsley and a generous amount of pepper, and serve at once.

Note: This dish includes eggs that are only partially cooked. For more information, see page 114.

MAKES 6 SERVINGS

PANCETTA

This flavorful bacon, which derives its name from *pancia*, Italian for "belly," is made by rubbing a slab of pork belly with a mix of spices that may include cinnamon, cloves, and juniper berries, then usually rolling the slab into a tight cylinder. The pancetta is then cured for at least 2 months. When the cylinder is cut, the slices of pancetta display a distinctive spiral of lean, satiny meat and pure white fat. In Italy, chopped pancetta sautéed in olive oil is used to flavor soups, fillings, sauces, braises, and side dishes.

GNOCCHI WITH QUATTRO FORMAGGI

PURÉEING POTATOES

Gnocchi are soft dumplings, often made with potatoes. A ricer or a food mill is ideal for puréeing the potatoes. Each tool treats them more gently than a food processor (which makes them gummy) and also separates out the peels. If using a ricer, place the cooked potatoes in the small perforated pot and press the plunger against the potatoes to force them through the holes. A food mill, which looks like a saucepan with an interior crank-shaped handle, will give similar results. For this recipe, use the disk with the largest holes.

To make the gnocchi, in a large saucepan, combine the potatoes with water to cover generously. Bring to a boil over high heat, reduce the heat to medium, and cook until tender when pierced with the tip of a knife, 10–12 minutes. Drain the potatoes and press through a potato ricer or a food mill fitted with the large disk set over a large bowl (*left*). Add the flour and eggs to the bowl and mix until well combined.

Turn the potato mixture out onto a lightly floured work surface. Dust your hands with flour and knead the mixture until soft and smooth, 2–3 minutes. Divide into 4 equal pieces and roll each into a rope, about ½ inch (12 mm) in diameter, dusting your hands again with flour if necessary. Cut the ropes into 1-inch (2.5-cm) pieces. Press one side of each piece against the tines of a fork or a nutmeg grater to make indentations. Set aside on a lightly floured surface until ready to cook.

Bring a large pot of water to a boil. Meanwhile, to make the sauce, combine the cream, fontina, and Gorgonzola in a saucepan. Warm slowly over low heat, stirring constantly, until the cheeses melt, 3–4 minutes. Stir in the ricotta, Parmesan, thyme, and salt and pepper to taste. Remove from the heat and keep warm.

Generously salt the boiling water, add the gnocchi, and cook until they rise to the surface, about 3 minutes. Using a slotted spoon, transfer the gnocchi to warmed bowls. Ladle the sauce over the top and, if desired, sprinkle with minced thyme and pepper. Serve at once.

MAKES 6 SERVINGS

FOR THE GNOCCHI:

1¾ lb (875 g) russet potatoes, peeled and cut into 2-inch (5-cm) chunks

1½ cups (7½ oz/235 g) unbleached all-purpose (plain) flour, plus extra for dusting

2 large eggs

FOR THE QUATTRO FORMAGGI SAUCE:

½ cup (4 fl oz/125 ml) heavy (double) cream

½ cup (2 oz/60 g) shredded fontina cheese

¼ cup (1 oz/30 g) crumbled Gorgonzola cheese

¼ cup (2 oz/60 g) whole-milk ricotta cheese

¼ cup (1 oz/30 g) freshly grated Parmesan cheese

½ teaspoon minced fresh thyme, plus extra for optional garnish

Salt and freshly ground pepper

BUTTERNUT SQUASH RAVIOLI

FOR THE SQUASH FILLING:

1 butternut squash, about 1½ lb (750 g)

¼ cup (½ oz/15 g) fresh bread crumbs (page 113)

1 large egg yolk

¼ cup (1 oz/30 g) freshly grated Parmesan cheese

Salt and freshly ground pepper

Pinch of freshly grated nutmeg

1 lb (500 g) pasta dough (page 110)

1 large egg beaten with 1 teaspoon water

FOR THE BUTTER AND SAGE SAUCE:

½ cup (4 oz/125 g) unsalted butter

40–50 small fresh sage leaves

¾ cup (3 oz/90 g) freshly grated Parmesan cheese (optional)

Freshly grated nutmeg (optional)

To make the squash filling, preheat the oven to 400°F (200°C). Line a baking sheet with parchment (baking) paper.

Cut the butternut squash in half lengthwise. Scoop out the seeds and discard. Place on the prepared baking sheet, cut side down, and bake until very soft when pierced with the tip of a knife, 35–45 minutes. Let cool to the touch. Peel the squash and purée the flesh in a food processor. Add the bread crumbs, egg yolk, and Parmesan and pulse to blend. Season with salt, pepper, and nutmeg and pulse to combine. Set aside.

To assemble the ravioli, roll out the pasta dough as directed on page 110. Place a pasta sheet on a lightly floured work surface. Spoon 1 tablespoon squash filling onto the pasta at 2-inch (5-cm) intervals. Using your finger or a pastry brush, lightly dampen the edges of the pasta sheet and the spaces between the filling with the egg wash. Top with a second pasta sheet and press with your fingers along the edges and around each mound of filling to seal and remove air bubbles. Cut into squares with a straight-edged pastry wheel or sharp, thin-bladed knife, then press the edges to secure. Make sure the filling does not break the seal, or the ravioli will come apart during cooking.

Bring a large pot of water to a boil. Meanwhile, to make the sauce, in a saucepan over medium heat, melt the butter. Add the sage and cook without stirring until the leaves crisp slightly and infuse the butter, 2–3 minutes. Remove from the heat and keep warm.

Generously salt the boiling water, add the ravioli, and cook until al dente, about 3 minutes. Drain well, place in a warmed large, shallow bowl, top with the sauce and Parmesan, if using, and toss gently to coat. Sprinkle with nutmeg, if desired. Serve at once.

MAKES 6 SERVINGS

SAGE

A perennial that grows profusely in Italy, sage has aromatic, soft, gray-green leaves. In Roman times, the pungent herb was valued for its medicinal properties. Today, its chief use is in the kitchen to season many dishes, including such classic recipes as chicken livers sautéed in butter. It also pairs well with other meats, especially veal and pork (page 64). Infusing butter with the flavor of sage, as for the sauce in this recipe, is a common northern Italian preparation for ravioli and tortellini.

CANNELLONI WITH BESCIAMELLA SAUCE

BESCIAMELLA SAUCE

To make this Italian version of French béchamel sauce, heat 2½ cups (20 fl oz/625 ml) whole milk in a saucepan over medium heat until small bubbles appear at the edge of the pan. In another saucepan, melt 3 tablespoons unsalted butter over medium heat. Whisk in 3 tablespoons all-purpose (plain) flour and cook, stirring, until foamy, 1–2 minutes. Whisk in the hot milk and cook, whisking constantly, until thickened, 3–4 minutes. Season with salt, freshly ground white pepper, and a pinch of freshly grated nutmeg.

To make the filling, in a large sauté pan over medium heat, heat the olive oil. Add the pancetta, onion, carrot, and celery and sauté until the onion is golden, about 5 minutes. Add the garlic and ground beef and cook, stirring to break up the meat, until the beef is lightly browned, 8–10 minutes. Add the tomatoes and cook until the mixture is thickened, about 15 minutes. Remove from the heat and let cool for 10–15 minutes. Stir in the egg yolks and ½ cup Parmesan. Season with salt and pepper. Set aside.

Roll out the pasta dough as directed on page 110. Using a straight-edged pastry wheel or a sharp, thin-bladed knife, cut into eight 4-by-6-inch (10-by-15-cm) rectangles. You will need 8 rectangles.

Bring a large pot of water to a boil. Lightly oil a baking sheet.

Generously salt the boiling water, add the pasta, a few rectangles at a time, and cook until al dente, about 3 minutes. Using a sieve, remove the pasta from the pot, drain well, and place on the prepared baking sheet in a single layer.

Preheat the oven to 375°F (190°C). To assemble the cannelloni, pour one-third of the *besciamella* sauce into a 9-inch (23-cm) square baking dish. Put ¼ cup (2 fl oz/60 ml) filling on each pasta rectangle and spread to cover the pasta, leaving a ¼-inch (6-mm) border around the edge. Working from one short side, roll up the pasta and filling. Place seam side down on top of the sauce in the baking dish. Repeat with the remaining pasta and filling, placing the rolls touching in a single layer. Pour the remaining *besciamella* sauce evenly over the cannelloni and sprinkle evenly with the ¼ cup Parmesan. Bake until the cheese is lightly browned, about 15 minutes.

Place 2 rolls on each individual plate and serve at once.

MAKES 4 SERVINGS

FOR THE FILLING:

2 tablespoons extra-virgin olive oil

1 oz (30 g) pancetta (page 51), finely chopped

¼ cup (1 oz/30 g) finely chopped yellow onion

1 carrot, peeled and shredded

1 celery stalk, finely chopped

1 clove garlic, finely chopped

1 lb (500 g) ground (minced) beef

4 plum (Roma) tomatoes, peeled and seeded (page 47), then chopped

2 large egg yolks

½ cup (2 oz/60 g) freshly grated Parmesan cheese

Salt and freshly ground pepper

1 lb (500 g) pasta dough (page 110)

Besciamella sauce *(far left)*

¼ cup (1 oz/30 g) freshly grated Parmesan cheese

MAIN COURSES

In Italy, main courses are as varied—and as splendid—as the landscape. Yet whether you are sitting down to Sicilian swordfish strewn with currants and pine nuts, Roman veal medallions layered with prosciutto and sage, or Tuscan roast chicken sauced with the local vin santo *wine, the dish will reflect the Italian insistence on only the best ingredients simply prepared.*

CHICKEN WITH VIN SANTO SAUCE
60

SWORDFISH WITH CURRANTS, OLIVES,
CAPERS, AND PINE NUTS
63

SALTIMBOCCA ALLA ROMANA
64

BRAISED PORK LOIN WITH PRUNES
67

ROAST SEA BASS WITH FENNEL AND LEMON
68

GRILLED VEAL CHOPS WITH BALSAMIC SAUCE
71

BRASATO AL BAROLO
72

RABBIT WITH ROASTED GARLIC
75

CHICKEN WITH VIN SANTO SAUCE

VIN SANTO

This sweet, amber dessert wine has a slightly caramel flavor with hints of almond and fig. White wine grapes selected for *vin santo* are left drying on the vine to allow the sugars to concentrate, and are further dried on rush mats in large, airy rooms. The wine is aged in small barrels for three or four years in a place where it is exposed to the great fluctuations in temperature necessary to form the distinctive character for which the wine is known. Revered as the wine of hospitality, *vin santo* is also used in sauces, risottos, and desserts.

Preheat the oven to 400°F (200°C). Lightly oil a roasting pan. In a small bowl, combine the parsley, thyme, and garlic. Rinse the chicken and pat dry. Using your fingers and beginning at the cavity, gently loosen the skin on both sides of the breast, working your fingers toward the neck and being careful not to tear the skin. Gently insert the parsley mixture under the skin, distributing it evenly. Pat the skin firmly back in place. Rub the skin with the olive oil and season the skin and cavity with salt and pepper. If desired, truss the chicken, tying the legs together with kitchen string. Tuck the wings under the back.

Place the chicken on one side in the prepared roasting pan. Roast for 10 minutes. Remove from the oven, turn the chicken on its other side, and roast for 10 minutes. Remove from the oven and turn breast side up. Continue to roast until browned, the juices run clear when a thigh is pierced with a fork, and an instant-read thermometer inserted into the thickest part of a thigh (away from the bone) registers 170°F (77°C), about 15 minutes longer.

Transfer the chicken to a warmed platter. Let rest, covered loosely with aluminum foil, for 10–15 minutes.

Skim the fat from the juices remaining in the roasting pan and discard. Place the pan on the stove top over medium-high heat. Add the *vin santo* and deglaze the pan, stirring to scrape up the browned bits from the pan bottom. Raise the heat to high and cook to reduce the sauce by half, 4–5 minutes. Remove from the heat and keep warm.

Carve the chicken. Drizzle the sauce over the chicken and serve.

Serving Tip: Roasted red potatoes make a good accompaniment. Halve the potatoes, toss with olive oil, fresh rosemary leaves, salt, and pepper, and roast in a separate dish while the chicken cooks.

MAKES 2–4 SERVINGS

2 tablespoons minced fresh flat-leaf (Italian) parsley

1 teaspoon minced fresh thyme

1 clove garlic, minced

1 small chicken, about 2 lb (1 kg)

3 tablespoons extra-virgin olive oil

Salt and freshly ground pepper

2 cups (16 fl oz/500 ml) *vin santo*

60

SWORDFISH WITH CURRANTS, OLIVES, CAPERS, AND PINE NUTS

6 swordfish steaks, about 2 lb (1 kg) total weight, each about 1 inch (2.5 cm) thick

3 tablespoons extra-virgin olive oil

1 yellow onion, thinly sliced

4 cloves garlic

1 cup (8 fl oz/250 ml) dry white wine

2 ripe tomatoes, peeled and seeded (page 47), then coarsely chopped

½ cup (2½ oz/75 g) oil-cured black olives, pitted and coarsely chopped

¼ cup (1½ oz/45 g) dried currants

Salt and freshly ground pepper

2 tablespoons salt-cured capers (page 32), rinsed and drained

2 tablespoons pine nuts, toasted (far right)

Preheat the oven to 400°F (200°C). Lightly oil a baking dish large enough to hold the swordfish steaks in a single layer. Place the steaks in the prepared dish.

In a large sauté pan over medium heat, heat the olive oil. Add the onion and garlic and sauté until softened but not browned, 2–3 minutes. Add the wine, tomatoes, olives, and currants and stir to combine. Season with salt and pepper and pour evenly over the swordfish.

Cover and bake until the swordfish is firm and opaque throughout, 15–20 minutes.

Transfer to a warmed serving platter and sprinkle with the capers and pine nuts and a grinding of pepper, if desired. Serve at once.

MAKES 6 SERVINGS

PINE NUTS

Known in Italy as *pinoli* or *pignoli*, pine nuts are harvested from a specific variety of stone pine. The small nuts have an elongated, slightly tapered shape and a delicate, resinous flavor. Like most nuts, pine nuts intensify in flavor and gain a crisp texture when toasted. To toast the nuts, place them in a dry frying pan over medium heat. Toast, stirring frequently, until the nuts are golden. Transfer at once to a plate and let cool before using. The nuts will continue to toast; therefore, cook them just a shade lighter than desired.

SALTIMBOCCA ALLA ROMANA

Place each veal cutlet between 2 pieces of parchment (baking) paper and set on a work surface. Using a rolling pin, roll to an even thickness of about ¼ inch (6 mm). Remove the top sheet of paper and cut each cutlet in half. Arrange a slice of prosciutto on each cutlet half, folding it to fit if necessary, and top the prosciutto with 2 sage leaves. Secure with toothpicks, threading them through the layers. Repeat with remaining cutlets.

In a large sauté pan over medium heat, heat the olive oil. Add the garlic and sauté until softened but not browned, 1–2 minutes. Add the spinach and sauté until the spinach is wilted and all of its rinsing water has evaporated, 5–7 minutes. Season to taste with salt and pepper. Transfer to a serving platter and keep warm.

Just before serving, in a sauté pan large enough to hold the veal in a single layer, melt the butter over medium heat until it foams. Add the veal, prosciutto side down, and cook until lightly browned on one side, about 1 minute. Using a spatula, turn and cook on the second side until lightly browned, about 1 minute. Add the lemon juice to the pan and season the sauce to taste with salt and pepper.

Arrange the veal on top of the spinach and remove the toothpicks. Serve at once, placing 2 pieces of veal and a portion of the spinach on each individual plate and drizzling with the sauce.

MAKES 4 SERVINGS

4 veal cutlets, about 5 oz (155 g) each

8 thin slices prosciutto

16 fresh sage leaves

3 tablespoons extra-virgin olive oil

1 clove garlic, minced

1 lb (500 g) spinach, stems removed and leaves well rinsed and chopped

Salt and freshly ground pepper

3 tablespoons unsalted butter

Juice of 1 lemon

PROSCIUTTO

This uncooked and unsmoked Italian ham, cut from the rear leg of pork, is cured with a minimum of salt for a month, then air-dried for 6 months to 2 years. The prosciutto develops a deep pink hue, subtle sweet-salty taste, and velvety texture. Prosciutto from Parma in the region of Emilia-Romagna is regarded as the best. In general, prosciutto is sliced paper-thin and eaten raw (crudo) or is only lightly cooked, since cooking can toughen the meat. Prosciutto is essential to this classic veal preparation and is a common offering on the antipasto platter.

BRAISED PORK LOIN WITH PRUNES

1 boneless pork loin, about 2 lb (1 kg), trimmed

Salt and freshly ground pepper

Unbleached all-purpose (plain) flour for dredging

¼ cup (2 fl oz/60 ml) extra-virgin olive oil

½ cup (2½ oz/75 g) finely chopped yellow onion

1 cup (8 fl oz/250 ml) dry white wine

2 cups (12 oz/375 g) pitted prunes

Cut the pork loin crosswise into 6 equal pieces. Season with salt and pepper. Dredge each piece in the flour to coat lightly, shaking off the excess.

In a sauté pan large enough to hold the pork in a single layer, heat the olive oil over medium-high heat. Add the onion and sauté until softened, about 2 minutes. Add the pork and cook until lightly browned, 3–4 minutes. Turn and cook on the second side until lightly browned, 3–4 minutes.

Add the wine and distribute the prunes evenly in the pan. Reduce the heat to medium-low, cover, and cook until the pork is tender when pierced with a fork and the sauce has thickened slightly, 15–20 minutes. Serve at once.

MAKES 6 SERVINGS

FRUIT VARIATIONS

The mildly sweet taste of pork lends itself well to braising with fruit, a pairing that is centuries old. Other fruits, dried or fresh, may be used in place of the prunes. Add 2 cups (12 oz/375 g) pitted dried apricots to the liquid after deglazing the pan. Or substitute 2 apples, such as Granny Smith or pippin, or 2 pears, such as Bosc or Bartlett (Williams'). Peel, halve, and core the apples or pears, cut into ¼-inch (6-mm) wedges, then add the fruit to the pan with the wine.

ROAST SEA BASS WITH FENNEL AND LEMON

Preheat the oven to 400°F (200°C). Cut off the stems and feathery leaves from the fennel bulb (reserve the feathery fronds to use as a garnish, if desired). Discard the outer layer of the bulb if it is tough and cut away any discolored areas. Halve the bulb lengthwise and cut out the solid core at the bottom of the bulb. Thinly slice each half crosswise.

In a roasting pan large enough to hold the sea bass steaks in a single layer, combine the fennel, potato, and onion slices. Drizzle with 3 tablespoons of the olive oil and toss to coat the vegetables. Season with salt and pepper. Spread the vegetables evenly in the pan and roast until light golden brown and tender when pierced with a fork, about 20 minutes.

Remove the roasting pan from the oven and place the sea bass on top of the vegetables in a single layer. Brush with the remaining 1 tablespoon olive oil. Sprinkle with the lemon zest and season with salt and pepper. Roast until the sea bass is firm and opaque throughout, about 10 minutes.

Transfer the sea bass and vegetables to individual plates or a platter and serve at once, garnished with the fennel fronds, if using.

MAKES 6 SERVINGS

1 fennel bulb

2 lb (1 kg) red potatoes, scrubbed and cut into slices 1 inch (2.5 cm) thick

1 yellow onion, sliced

4 tablespoons (2 fl oz/ 60 ml) extra-virgin olive oil

Salt and freshly ground pepper

6 sea bass steaks, about 2 lb (1 kg) total weight

Finely grated zest of 1 lemon

GRILLED VEAL CHOPS WITH BALSAMIC SAUCE

4 tablespoons (2 fl oz/
60 ml) extra-virgin olive oil

4 veal chops, each about
6 oz (185 g) and ¾ inch
(2 cm) thick

Salt and freshly ground
pepper

¼ cup (1½ oz/45 g) finely
chopped yellow onion

½ cup (4 fl oz/125 ml)
balsamic vinegar

2 cups (16 fl oz/500 ml)
meat stock (page 111)

2 tablespoons unsalted
butter

Chopped fresh flat-leaf
(Italian) parsley for garnish
(optional)

Prepare a charcoal fire in an outdoor grill and let burn until the coals are covered with white ash. Leave the coals heaped in the center of the grill; do not spread them out. For a gas grill, preheat on high heat. Brush the grill rack with olive oil.

Brush both sides of the veal chops with 1 tablespoon of the olive oil. Season with salt and pepper. Using tongs (to avoid piercing the meat), place the chops on the rack and grill, turning once, until browned, 4–6 minutes per side for medium. Place on a serving platter and keep warm.

In a saucepan over medium-high heat, warm the remaining 3 tablespoons oil. Add the onion and sauté until golden, 3–4 minutes. Add the balsamic vinegar, raise the heat to high, and cook until reduced by half, 4–5 minutes. Add the stock and cook until the liquid is reduced by half, 10–12 minutes. Whisk in the butter and season to taste with salt and pepper.

Divide the chops among individual plates, spoon the sauce over the chops, garnish with the parsley, if desired, and serve at once.

MAKES 4 SERVINGS

POLENTA

Silken polenta, cooked Italian cornmeal, makes the perfect complement for this veal bathed in a sauce flavored with balsamic vinegar. Seek out stone-ground cornmeal for the best results. In a large saucepan over medium-high heat, bring 5 cups (40 fl oz/ 1.25 l) water to a boil. Whisking constantly, add 1½ cups (7½ oz/235 g) fine-ground polenta in a slow, steady stream. Stir in ½ teaspoon salt, reduce the heat to medium-low, and continue to cook, stirring constantly, until the polenta thickens and pulls away from the sides of the pan, about 20 minutes.

BRASATO AL BAROLO

Compress the meat into a cylindrical shape and tie with kitchen string at 1- to 2-inch (2.5- to 5-cm) intervals along its length. Place in a large nonaluminum pot and add the wine. Place the garlic, cloves, 1 rosemary sprig, and bay leaf on a square of cheesecloth (muslin), gather the corners, and tie with kitchen string to make a bundle. Add to the pot and turn the meat to coat with the marinade. Cover and refrigerate for at least 2 hours or up to overnight, turning the meat occasionally. Drain the meat, reserving the marinade and the cheesecloth bundle. Preheat the oven to 375°F (190°C).

In a Dutch oven or large roasting pan over medium-high heat, heat the olive oil. Add the onion, celery, and carrots and sauté until the onion is golden, 3–4 minutes. Add the roast and cook, turning as needed, until browned on all sides, 6–8 minutes. Add the reserved marinade and cheesecloth bundle, and season with salt and pepper. Cover and roast until the meat is tender when pierced with a fork, about 2 hours.

Remove from the oven and transfer the roast to a platter. Cover loosely with aluminum foil while finishing the sauce.

Remove and discard the cheesecloth bundle from the pan. Pour the contents of the pan into a fine-mesh sieve set over a bowl. Return the vegetables and 2 cups (16 fl oz/500 ml) of the pan juices to the roasting pan. Place over high heat and cook the juices until reduced and thickened, 10–12 minutes. If desired, transfer part or all of the sauce to a blender or food processor and purée until smooth, then return to the pan to heat through.

Cut the meat across the grain into slices, arrange on the platter, and spoon the sauce on top. Garnish with rosemary and serve at once.

MAKES 6 SERVINGS

2 lb (1 kg) boneless veal or beef rump or loin

1 bottle (750 ml) red wine *(far left)*

2 cloves garlic, minced

2 whole cloves

1 fresh rosemary sprig, plus extra for garnish

1 bay leaf

3 tablespoons extra-virgin olive oil

1 yellow onion, chopped

2 celery stalks, chopped

2 carrots, peeled and chopped

Salt and freshly ground pepper

RABBIT WITH ROASTED GARLIC

1 rabbit (see Note), about 3 lb (1.5 kg), cut into 8 serving pieces

1 lemon

1 orange

2 cups (16 fl oz/500 ml) dry white wine

1 fresh rosemary sprig

2 cloves garlic

5 juniper berries

¼ cup (2 fl oz/60 ml) extra-virgin olive oil

Salt and freshly ground pepper

4 heads roasted garlic (far right)

Rinse the rabbit pieces well and set aside. Remove the zest from the lemon and orange in fine strips. Juice the lemon and orange and put the juices in a large nonaluminum bowl. Add the wine, zest, rosemary, garlic, and juniper berries. Add the rabbit pieces, turn to coat with the marinade, cover, and marinate for at least 30 minutes or up to 1 hour at room temperature, or overnight in the refrigerator, turning the meat occasionally. Drain, reserving the marinade and seasonings.

In a large frying pan over medium-high heat, warm the olive oil. Add the rabbit pieces and cook, turning once, until browned on both sides, 8–10 minutes total. Add the reserved marinade and seasonings, cover partially, and cook, turning once, until the rabbit is tender when pierced with a fork, 20–30 minutes. Season to taste with salt and pepper.

Transfer the rabbit pieces and sauce to a serving platter and arrange the roasted garlic alongside. Each diner is given a head of garlic, along with a portion of rabbit and sauce. Diners squeeze the roasted cloves over the rabbit as desired.

Note: Rabbit is much more common in European markets than in American ones, but any quality butcher shop should be able to order one for you, as well as cut it into serving pieces for use in this recipe.

Serving Tip: The rabbit and sauce are delicious served with polenta (page 71). Ladle the polenta on individual plates, top with the rabbit, and moisten with the sauce. Serve the roasted garlic on the side.

MAKES 4 SERVINGS

ROASTING GARLIC

Preheat the oven to 300°F (150°C). Using a small, sharp knife, score 4 heads of garlic around the middle without cutting into the cloves. Remove the top half of the papery skin, exposing the cloves. Place the heads in a small, lightly oiled roasting pan and drizzle with ½ cup (4 fl oz/125 ml) olive oil. Season with salt and pepper, cover with aluminum foil, and roast for 1 hour. Uncover and roast, basting frequently with the pan juices, until the heads are tender when pierced with a knife, 10–15 minutes longer.

VEGETABLES

Italian cooks traditionally rely on locally cultivated vegetables for the table, harvested either from their own gardens or from the fields of nearby farms. This respect for the seasons finds tomatoes and eggplants (aubergines) prepared in summertime, at their peak of flavor, while broccoli rabe, fennel, and leafy greens star in cooler weather.

GRILLED VEGETABLES

RADICCHIO

Radicchio is a member of the chicory family, a large group of bitter greens that grows wild throughout Italy. Many types of radicchio are now cultivated.

One variety is *radicchio di Treviso*, characterized by long, narrow, mostly white or light green leaves with red tips. Another is the round *radicchio di Verona*, which has reddish purple leaves on creamy white stems and may be substituted if Treviso is unavailable. Both varieties are crisp and bittersweet and are enjoyed raw in salads or cooked. Grilling the radicchio mellows the slight bitterness of the leaves.

Prepare a charcoal fire in an outdoor grill and let burn until the coals are covered with white ash. Spread the coals in an even layer. For a gas grill, preheat on high heat. Brush the grill rack with olive oil.

Trim the ends from each eggplant, then cut lengthwise into slices ½ inch (12 mm) thick. Discard the 2 outer slices, which will be mostly skin. Lightly brush the eggplants, radicchio, bell peppers, zucchini, and mushrooms with olive oil. Season lightly with salt and pepper.

Using tongs and working in batches if necessary, place the vegetables on the rack and grill, turning once, until lightly browned, 3–4 minutes per side.

Transfer the grilled vegetables to a platter and serve hot or at room temperature.

Note: Italian eggplants are longer and thinner than the globe eggplants found in most markets. If they are unavailable, substitute Asian eggplants, which are also long and slender.

MAKES 6 SERVINGS

Extra-virgin olive oil as needed

2 Italian eggplants (aubergines) (see Note)

2 heads Treviso radicchio, quartered lengthwise

1 red bell pepper (capsicum), seeded and cut lengthwise into eighths

1 yellow bell pepper (capsicum), seeded and cut lengthwise into eighths

2 small zucchini (courgettes), trimmed and sliced crosswise on the diagonal

6 large fresh white or cremini mushrooms, caps brushed clean

Salt and freshly ground pepper

SPINACH TIMBALES

1 lb (500 g) spinach, stems removed and leaves well rinsed

3 large egg yolks, lightly beaten

½ cup (4 fl oz/125 ml) whole milk

½ cup (2 oz/60 g) freshly grated Parmesan cheese, plus extra for sprinkling

Pinch of freshly grated nutmeg

Salt and freshly ground pepper

Preheat the oven to 350°F (180°C). Lightly butter four ½-cup (4–fl oz/125-ml) ramekins.

Put the spinach with the rinsing water still clinging to the leaves in a saucepan over medium-high heat, cover, and cook until the spinach is bright green and wilted, 1–2 minutes. Drain and rinse under running cold water. When the spinach is cool enough to handle, form it into a ball and squeeze out as much water as possible. Finely chop the spinach and place in a bowl.

Add the egg yolks, milk, and Parmesan to the bowl and stir well to combine. Season with the nutmeg and salt and pepper. Divide the spinach mixture among the prepared ramekins. Place the ramekins in a large baking pan and pour hot tap water into the pan to reach halfway up the sides of the ramekins. Carefully place the pan in the oven and bake until a knife inserted in the center of a timbale comes out clean, 55–60 minutes.

Carefully remove the baking pan from the oven and transfer the ramekins to a wire rack to cool for 10 minutes.

To unmold the timbales, run a knife around the inside edge of each ramekin, invert a plate on the ramekin, and invert the ramekin and plate together. Lift off the ramekin. Repeat with the remaining ramekins. Serve the timbales warm or at room temperature, sprinkled with Parmesan.

Serving Tip: The timbales make an excellent accompaniment for veal chops (page 71) or rabbit (page 75). Or, serve them with saltimbocca (page 64) in place of the bed of spinach.

MAKES 4 SERVINGS

TIMBALE VARIATIONS

The term for this savory dish (spelled *timballi* in Italian) is derived from the French word for kettledrum, an apt description of timbales when removed from their molds. Other vegetables may be used in place of the spinach. Rinse 1 lb (500 g) Swiss chard leaves, remove the tough stems, and prepare as for the spinach. To substitute zucchini (courgettes) or carrots, cut them into ½-inch (12-mm) pieces, then steam until tender, about 8–10 minutes. Purée in a food processor with 2 tablespoons of the cooking liquid. You will need 1½ cups (12 fl oz/375 ml) purée.

81

BROCCOLI RABE WITH SPICY OLIVE OIL DRESSING

In a small saucepan, combine the olive oil, onion, and red pepper flakes. Bring to a simmer over low heat and cook for 5 minutes. Remove from the heat and let cool.

Have ready a large bowl of ice water. Bring a large saucepan three-fourths full of salted water to a boil. Add the broccoli rabe and cook until bright green and slightly softened, about 1 minute. Drain and immediately immerse in the ice water to halt the cooking. Drain again, pat dry, and set aside.

Peel and section the blood oranges *(left)*. Add the broccoli rabe to the bowl with the oranges and set aside.

Put the vinegar in a small glass bowl. Strain the oil and discard the onion slices and red pepper flakes. Whisking constantly, gradually drizzle the seasoned oil into the vinegar. Season to taste with salt and black pepper.

Pour the dressing over the orange segments and broccoli rabe and toss to coat well. Serve at room temperature.

MAKES 6 SERVINGS

½ cup (4 fl oz/125 ml) extra-virgin olive oil

½ red onion, thinly sliced

1 teaspoon red pepper flakes, or to taste

1 lb (500 g) broccoli rabe (page 44), trimmed and cut into 3-inch (7.5-cm) pieces

8 small blood oranges

2 tablespoons red wine vinegar

Salt and freshly ground black pepper

PREPARING
BLOOD ORANGES

Winter marks the arrival in markets of these oranges with their distinctive blood-red flesh and sweet juice. To prepare the oranges for this recipe, cut a slice off the top and bottom of each orange, then stand it upright on a cutting board. Following the contours of the fruit, slice off the peel and white pith in thick strips. Holding the fruit over a bowl, carefully cut along both sides of the membranes between the sections, letting each freed section and any juices drop into the bowl.

ROASTED POTATOES WITH FENNEL AND ONION

2 lb (1 kg) russet potatoes, peeled and cut into 2-inch (5-cm) chunks

1 yellow onion, cut lengthwise into eighths

1 fennel bulb, trimmed *(far right)* and cut lengthwise into eighths

¼ cup (2 fl oz/60 ml) extra-virgin olive oil

Salt and freshly ground pepper

Preheat the oven to 400°F (200°C).

In a roasting pan, combine the potatoes, onion, and fennel. Drizzle the vegetables with the olive oil and toss well to coat. Spread them in a single layer and season with salt and pepper.

Roast, turning occasionally, until the vegetables are golden brown and tender when pierced with the tip of a knife, about 30 minutes.

Remove from the oven, transfer to a serving dish, and serve at once.

Serving Tip: Offer the vegetables alongside roasted or grilled meats such as chicken (page 60), veal (page 71), or beef (page 21).

MAKES 6 SERVINGS

PREPARING FENNEL

Called *finocchio* in Italy, fennel has a base that swells to a bulb of ribbed layers from which slimmer stems emerge. A native of the Mediterranean region, it has a faint licorice flavor and a crisp texture. Select creamy-colored bulbs topped by fresh-looking stems and feathery green tops. To prepare a bulb, cut off the stems and leaves and discard or reserve for another use. Peel away the tough outer layer of the bulb. Trim away the base of the core if it is thick and discolored and cut the bulb as directed in the recipe.

RICOTTA-STUFFED EGGPLANT ROLLS

Preheat the broiler (grill). Lightly oil a baking sheet and an 8-inch (20-cm) square baking dish.

Peel the eggplant and cut off the stem end. Stand the eggplant upright on the cut end and cut vertically into slices ¼ inch (6 mm) thick. You will need 8 slices. Salt the slices and let drain *(left)*.

Brush both sides of the slices with 2 tablespoons of the olive oil. Arrange on the prepared baking sheet, place in the broiler about 4 inches (10 cm) from the heat source, and broil (grill) the slices until lightly browned on top, about 2 minutes. Remove the sheet from the broiler, turn the slices, return to the broiler, and broil until lightly browned on the second side, about 2 minutes. Set aside to cool. Reduce the oven temperature to 375°F (190°C).

In a sauté pan over medium heat, heat the remaining 6 table-spoons (3 fl oz/90 ml) oil. Add the garlic and sauté until softened, about 2 minutes. Add the tomatoes, basil, and parsley and cook until slightly thickened, 15–20 minutes. Season with salt and pepper. Transfer to a blender or food processor and purée until smooth. Pour half of the sauce into the prepared baking dish.

Place 1 heaping tablespoon of ricotta on each eggplant slice and spread to cover the slice, leaving a ½-inch (12-mm) border. Beginning at a narrow end, roll the slice to enclose the cheese. Place the rolls seam side down on top of the tomato sauce in a single layer. Evenly cover the rolls with the remaining tomato sauce. Sprinkle with the Parmesan, distributing it evenly. Bake until the sauce is bubbling hot and the cheese is golden brown, 30–35 minutes. Remove from the oven and serve at once.

MAKES 4 SERVINGS

SALTING EGGPLANT

Salting the eggplant slices and letting them sit for a time draws out their bitter juices and drains excess moisture that would otherwise cause the filling for these rolled egg-plant slices to become watery. After peeling and slicing the eggplant, lightly sprinkle both sides of the slices with salt. Set the slices on a wire rack in a baking pan or in a colander over a plate. Let stand for about 30 minutes. Wipe the slices with paper towels to remove excess salt; do not rinse the slices under running water, as the eggplant will absorb the water.

1 large eggplant (aubergine), about 1 lb (500 g)

8 tablespoons (4 fl oz/ 125 ml) extra-virgin olive oil

2 cloves garlic, minced

6 large ripe tomatoes, peeled and seeded (page 47), then chopped

¼ cup (¼ oz/7 g) fresh basil leaves, minced

1 tablespoon minced fresh flat-leaf (Italian) parsley

Salt and freshly ground pepper

½ cup (4 oz/125 g) whole-milk ricotta cheese

½ cup (2 oz/60 g) freshly grated Parmesan cheese

DESSERTS

When special occasions are celebrated at home, Italians enjoy rich cream-filled cakes, elegant layered pastries, and other fancy desserts. But everyday family meals typically end with an assortment of seasonal fresh fruits or sometimes a plate of almond biscotti, scoops of icy granita, or a bowl of berries garnished with Marsala-infused zabaglione.

ALMOND BISCOTTI
90

PANNA COTTA WITH STRAWBERRIES
93

GELATO BACIO
94

ZABAGLIONE
97

ESPRESSO GRANITA
98

TIRAMISÙ
100

ALMOND BISCOTTI

Preheat the oven to 325°F (165°C). Line a baking sheet with parchment (baking) paper.

In a large bowl, combine the cake flour, all-purpose flour, baking powder, salt, and almonds. Stir to mix well.

In another bowl, using a handheld mixer on medium speed, beat the eggs and sugar until pale yellow and light in texture, about 2 minutes. Add the vanilla and orange extracts and orange zest and mix well. Add to the dry ingredients; stir just until blended. The dough will be soft and sticky.

Dust your hands with flour, transfer the dough to the prepared baking sheet, and form into a log 3–4 inches (7.5–10 cm) wide and about 12 inches (30 cm) long. Bake until a toothpick inserted into the center comes out clean, about 45 minutes. Using the parchment paper to lift the log, transfer it to a wire rack to cool for 15–20 minutes. Reduce the oven temperature to 275°F (135°C). Line the baking sheet with a new piece of parchment paper. Line a second baking sheet with paper.

Place the log on a cutting board and, using a long serrated knife, cut on the diagonal into slices ½ inch (12 mm) thick. Place the slices cut side down on the prepared baking sheets, spacing them about ½ inch (12 mm) apart. Bake the biscotti for 15 minutes. Remove the baking sheets from the oven, turn the biscotti, and bake until pale golden brown, 10–15 minutes longer. Transfer the biscotti to wire racks to cool. If not serving the biscotti immediately, store them in an airtight container for up to 2 weeks.

Variation Tip: Use 1 cup (5 oz/155 g) hazelnuts (filberts) in place of the almonds. Toast them as directed on page 94.

MAKES 24 BISCOTTI

TOASTING NUTS

Double baking makes biscotti (meaning "twice-baked") as crisp and durable as they are tasty, perfect for dunking in coffee or a sweet dessert wine such as *vin santo* (page 60). To toast the almonds for the biscotti or the walnuts for ravioli sauce (page 48), spread in a single layer on a rimmed baking sheet and bake in a preheated 350°F (180°C) oven, stirring occasionally, until the nuts are lightly browned and fragrant, about 10 minutes. Remove the nuts from the pan as soon as they start to look done, pour onto a plate, and let cool.

1½ cups (6 oz/185 g) cake (soft-wheat) flour

1½ cups (7½ oz/235 g) unbleached all-purpose (plain) flour, plus extra for dusting

1 teaspoon baking powder

¾ teaspoon salt

1 cup (5½ oz/170 g) whole almonds, toasted *(far left)*

4 large eggs

1 cup (8 oz/250 g) sugar

1½ teaspoons vanilla extract (essence)

½ teaspoon orange extract (essence)

1 tablespoon finely grated orange zest

PANNA COTTA WITH STRAWBERRIES

FOR THE PANNA COTTA:

2½ teaspoons unflavored powdered gelatin

2½ cups (20 fl oz/625 ml) heavy (double) cream

½ cup (4 fl oz/125 ml) whole milk

⅓ cup (3 oz/90 g) sugar

Pinch of salt

1 teaspoon vanilla extract (essence)

FOR THE STRAWBERRIES:

3 cups (12 oz/375 g) strawberries, hulled and cut into quarters

3 tablespoons sugar

1 teaspoon finely grated orange zest

To make the *panna cotta,* in a small bowl, sprinkle the gelatin over 3 tablespoons cold water and stir to blend. Let stand until the gelatin is softened, about 5 minutes.

Pour the cream and milk into a large saucepan. Add the sugar and salt, place over medium heat, and heat, stirring to dissolve the sugar, until bubbles appear along the edge of the pan. Stir in the gelatin mixture and remove from the heat. Set aside to cool slightly, stirring occasionally, about 10 minutes. Stir in the vanilla. Divide among six ¾-cup (6–fl oz/180-ml) ramekins. Cover and refrigerate for at least 6 hours or up to overnight.

To make the strawberries, combine the strawberries, sugar, zest, and 2 tablespoons water in a saucepan. Bring to a simmer over low heat and cook, stirring occasionally, until the berries are soft, 3–5 minutes. Remove from the heat. Let cool to room temperature, or cover and refrigerate for up to 6 hours.

To unmold the *panna cotta,* run a knife around the inside edge of each ramekin, invert a plate on the ramekin, and invert the plate and ramekin together. Lift off the ramekin.

Spoon the strawberries around the *panna cotta,* dividing them evenly, and serve at once.

MAKES 6 SERVINGS

USING GELATIN

This odorless, colorless, flavorless ingredient derived from animal protein is often employed to help thicken the various liquids used in making mousses, puddings, and other molded desserts, including this *panna cotta,* or "cooked cream." Two types of gelatin, powdered and leaf, are available. For this recipe, look for powdered gelatin packaged in small paper envelopes, each of which contains about 2½ teaspoons. When used in a recipe, gelatin needs to be softened in liquid such as the warm milk here.

GELATO BACIO

GELATO AFFOGATO

Affogato, literally "drowned," vividly describes a dessert made by pouring just-brewed espresso or liqueur over a scoop of gelato. The espresso softens the gelato and adds a bitter taste complement to the sweet and silky ice cream. The hazelnut gelato here may be served in the same way. Prepare about 1½ cups (12 fl oz/375 ml) espresso or strong coffee, preferably using freshly ground, dark-roasted coffee beans (page 98). Place scoops of gelato in glasses and, while the coffee is still hot, pour ¼ cup (2 fl oz/60 ml) over the gelato in each glass.

Preheat the oven to 375°F (190°C). Spread the hazelnuts on a baking pan. Toast, shaking the pan occasionally, until the nuts are golden brown and fragrant, 5–7 minutes. While the nuts are still warm, place them in a kitchen towel. Rub them together vigorously to remove most of the skins. Place the nuts in a food processor with ¼ cup (2 oz/60 g) of the sugar and pulse to chop finely; do not overprocess.

In a large saucepan over medium heat, combine the milk, ground hazelnuts, and salt. Heat until bubbles appear along the edge of the pan. Remove from the heat and let stand at room temperature for at least 30 minutes or up to 2 hours.

In a small saucepan, warm the cream over low heat. Remove from the heat and add the chocolate. Stir until melted and smooth. Add to the milk mixture in the large saucepan and stir to combine. Place over low heat to warm the mixture.

In a bowl, whisk together the remaining ½ cup (4 oz/125 g) sugar and the egg yolks until very thick and pale yellow, about 2 minutes. Whisking constantly, slowly pour ½ cup (4 fl oz/125 ml) of the warm milk mixture into the eggs. Pour the egg mixture into the saucepan. Cook over medium heat, stirring constantly with a wooden spoon, until the mixture is thick enough to coat the back of the spoon and leaves a clear trail when a finger is drawn through it, 5–7 minutes. Do not let boil. Remove from the heat and set the pan in a bowl partially filled with ice cubes and water. Stir the mixture until cool. Cover and refrigerate until cold, at least 4 hours or up to 24 hours.

Pour the mixture into an ice-cream maker and freeze according to the manufacturer's instructions. Transfer the gelato to a freezer-safe container, cover, and freeze until firm, about 2 hours.

MAKES 6 SERVINGS

1 cup (5 oz/155 g) hazelnuts (filberts)

¾ cup (6 oz/185 g) sugar

3 cups (24 fl oz/750 ml) whole milk

⅛ teaspoon salt

½ cup (4 fl oz/125 ml) heavy (double) cream

4½ oz (140 g) bittersweet or semisweet (plain) chocolate, chopped

4 large egg yolks

ZABAGLIONE

⅓ cup (3 oz/90 g) sugar

6 large egg yolks

2 cups (16 fl oz/500 ml) sweet Marsala

2–3 cups (8–12 oz/250–375 g) raspberries

In a heatproof bowl, whisk together the sugar and egg yolks until the sugar has dissolved and the mixture is pale yellow and light in texture, about 2 minutes. Continuing to whisk, gradually add the Marsala.

Place the bowl over a saucepan containing barely simmering water, or transfer to the top pan of a double boiler set over barely simmering water. Cook, whisking constantly, until the mixture thickens and has increased in volume, 8–10 minutes.

Divide the raspberries among dessert bowls, reserving a few berries for garnishing, and top with the zabaglione, dividing it evenly. Garnish with the berries and serve at once.

Variation Tips: Whole blackberries or blueberries or sliced strawberries may be used in place of the raspberries. When fresh figs are in season, remove the stems from 12 very ripe Mission or Calimyrna figs. Cut the figs lengthwise into quarters and divide among dessert plates, then top with zabaglione.

MAKES 6 SERVINGS

MAKING ZABAGLIONE

Zabaglione is thought to have been invented in sixteenth-century Florence, in the Medici court. The Italians call this light, foamy, warm custard a "spoon dessert" and serve it either by itself or as a sauce over fruit, cake, or ice cream. Marsala, an amber-colored, fortified Italian dessert wine, is the traditional flavoring ingredient. The eggs for zabaglione must be cooked very slowly in the top of a double boiler, rather than over direct heat, so that they do not curdle. The slow cooking and constant whisking ensure that the finished dessert will have a light, fluffy consistency.

ESPRESSO GRANITA

In a bowl, combine the espresso and sugar, stirring to dissolve the sugar. Set aside and let cool completely, about 30 minutes.

Pour the mixture into a 9-inch (23-cm) round or square metal pan. Place in the freezer until the mixture becomes icy around the edges, about 30 minutes. Remove from the freezer and stir gently with a fork to break up the ice crystals. Return to the freezer. Continue to freeze, stirring the mixture every 20 minutes, until it forms flakes, about 1 hour.

To serve, divide the granita among chilled aperitif or other glasses. The granita is best served shortly after making.

MAKES 6 SERVINGS

3 cups (24 fl oz/750 ml) freshly brewed espresso *(far left)*

½ cup (4 oz/125 g) sugar

MAKING COFFEE

The key to brewing good coffee is the coffee bean. Dark-roasted coffee beans, usually called Italian or French roast, produce full-bodied coffee and are also used for espresso. Buy the beans preground in small quantities. Make sure you start with cold tap water or bottled spring water. For granita with a pure, intense flavor, use an espresso maker. For a milder version, brew the coffee double strength in a drip coffeemaker. Measure 2 level tablespoons ground coffee for every ¾ cup (6 fl oz/180 ml) water.

TIRAMISÙ

In a small saucepan over medium heat, combine the sugar and ½ cup (4 fl oz/125 ml) water and cook, stirring frequently, until the sugar dissolves. Remove from the heat, stir in the espresso, and let cool to room temperature. When the espresso mixture has cooled, stir in the rum.

Pour the espresso mixture into a wide, shallow bowl. Working in batches, briefly immerse the ladyfingers in the liquid. Using a spatula, transfer the ladyfingers to a plate. Set aside.

To make the filling, in a heatproof bowl, whisk together the egg yolks and sugar until the sugar has dissolved and the mixture is pale yellow and light in texture, about 2 minutes. Place the bowl over a saucepan containing barely simmering water, or transfer to the top pan of a double boiler set over barely simmering water. Using a handheld mixer on medium speed, beat the yolk mixture until very thick, about 6 minutes. Remove from the heat and set aside to cool, stirring frequently.

Meanwhile, in a bowl, using the mixer on medium-high speed, beat the cream until stiff peaks form when the beaters are lifted.

(Continued on next page.)

½ cup (4 oz/125 g) sugar

2 cups (16 fl oz/500 ml) freshly brewed espresso (page 98)

3 tablespoons dark rum

45 ladyfingers or *savoiardi* (see Notes)

FOR THE FILLING:

6 large egg yolks

⅓ cup (3 oz/90 g) sugar

½ cup (4 fl oz/125 ml) heavy (double) cream

1½ cups (12 oz/375 g) mascarpone cheese

1½ teaspoons vanilla extract (essence)

Unsweetened cocoa powder for garnish

TIRAMISÙ

Various stories surround the origin of tiramisù. According to many sources, inspiration for the dessert may have come from the English, who introduced their dessert called the trifle to Tuscany more than a century ago. The foundation of the modern version of tiramisù is a sponge cake, sometimes in the form of ladyfingers, as in this recipe. The ladyfingers are bathed in espresso and spirits and arranged in layers between a filling enriched with mascarpone *(opposite)*. A dusting of cocoa or a garnish of chocolate shavings is the final embellishment.

Add the mascarpone and vanilla to the yolk mixture. Beat with the mixer on medium speed until smooth and well blended. Using a large rubber spatula, fold in the whipped cream.

To assemble, use a metal spatula to transfer 15 soaked ladyfingers to a 9-inch (23-cm) square cake pan. Arrange them in a single later in the bottom of the pan. Using the rubber spatula, evenly spread one-third of the filling over the ladyfingers. Place another layer of 15 ladyfingers over the filling in the pan and evenly spread with half of the remaining filling. Top with the remaining lady-fingers and filling, again spreading evenly.

Gently tap the pan against the counter to settle the ingredients. Cover with plastic wrap and refrigerate for at least 6 hours or up to overnight.

To serve, run a thin knife around the inside of the cake pan to loosen the cake. Sift a dusting of cocoa over the top. Cut into slices and serve.

Notes: Ladyfingers—light, flat cookies that are as long as a finger—are available in many food stores and bakeries. Savoiardi, the Italian version of these delicate sponge cakes, are sold in specialty-food stores and by mail order. This dish includes eggs that are only partially cooked. For more information, see page 114.

MAKES 8 SERVINGS

(Photograph appears on following page.)

MASCARPONE CHEESE

An essential ingredient in tiramisù, mascarpone is a very soft, smooth fresh Italian cheese made from cream, with a consistency much like that of sour cream. The cheese, when chilled, is thick enough to spread; when room temperature, it is sufficiently fluid to pour. Mascarpone is noted for its rich flavor and acidic tang. It is sold in plastic containers in Italian markets and some supermarkets.

ITALIAN BASICS

Everyday Italian cooking is remarkably simple, involving a handful of quality ingredients and straightforward cooking methods, yet the finished dishes are among the most flavorful in the world. This excellence is largely due to the use of local products—seasonal vegetables, artisanal cheeses, naturally grazed beef, fresh fish—and to a respect for tradition that is shaped both by history and by regional differences.

REGIONAL CUISINE

After centuries of shifting alliances and waves of invaders, Italy's diverse regions were finally united under one flag in 1861. Yet even now, more than 150 years later, these regional borders are defined not only by the national government, but also by language, custom, and, in particular, food.

Geography is one of the reasons for the sharp distinctions. The country's long, narrow silhouette, with the sea on three sides and the Alps across the top, embraces a mixture of terrains—rolling hills, high mountains, large flood plains—and microclimates that naturally divide the population. This inherent variety has prompted regions to produce foods unique to them such as the balsamic vinegar of

Emilia-Romagna, the olive oil of Liguria and Tuscany, the dried pasta of Abruzzo, the rice of Piedmont, the Chianina beef of Tuscany, and the citrus fruits of Sicily.

Each region of Italy has its local interpretations as well, both in use of ingredients and in style. For example, Italian cheeses are made from sheep's, cow's, or goat's milk, depending on what is raised locally. Cow's milk can be turned into cheeses as markedly different as the buttery fontina of the Aosta Valley and the hard, tangy Parmigiano-Reggiano of Emilia-Romagna. Indeed, types of Italian cheeses number over four hundred distinct regional flavors and shapes.

Economic conditions add yet another layer of influence. Affluent northern Italy is home to the Po River valley, one of country's most productive agricultural areas; good pastureland for cattle; and a vital industrial economy. This wealth is evident in the generous use of butter and other dairy products, meat, and the local rice. In contrast, much of the economy of the south is built on small-scale farming and fishing, and the dishes more often focus on seafood, pork, and the glorious local produce.

However, Italian cooks in every corner of the country insist that ingredients be not only regional, but also at their seasonal best. The traditional weekly market, usually held in the main square of a village or town, is a showcase of the local harvest. In autumn, vendors' bins brim with chestnuts, squashes, and porcino mushrooms, while springtime delivers a bounty of tender, young asparagus, peas, and tiny wild strawberries.

In the last ten years, supermarkets have made inroads into the Italian kitchen, introducing more foreign products and produce that is not locally in season. Traditions die hard, however, as Italy's most ubiquitous food, pasta, illustrates. The difference between dried and fresh pasta is largely defined by wheat variety. In the south, farmers cultivate hard semolina wheat, perfect for making the factory-produced extruded and dried pasta that is popular there. In the north, fields are sown with soft winter wheat, ideal for the delicate handmade fresh pastas of northern kitchens.

Seeking out artisanal ingredients will enhance your success in making the recipes in this book.

MAKING PASTA

Traditionally, pasta dough is prepared and rolled out by hand, but a food processor and a hand-cranked pasta machine will speed the task.

For making your own pasta, use high-quality ingredients. Seek out the freshest eggs and unbleached all-purpose (plain) flour. Even though you may find bags of semolina flour labeled "pasta flour," this hard wheat is too high in protein for most fresh pasta. Protein content determines how much gluten, or elasticity, a dough will develop. There is sufficient protein in all-purpose flour to deliver ample "stretch" and tender texture. Whether you are working by hand or with a food processor (see the pasta dough recipe, page 110), the dough should be smooth and neither sticky nor too dry. Once you start kneading, add flour in only very small amounts to correct the consistency.

To roll out pasta dough by hand, which produces a particularly delicate result with a slightly uneven texture, you will need a large wooden or marble surface and a long, slender rolling pin (Italians cooks use a pin more than a yard/meter long). If you opt for a pasta machine instead, it will do some additional kneading in the early stages of rolling and then produce a uniformly thin sheet.

Cut, fill, and shape stuffed pastas, such as ravioli, immediately, while the dough sheets are still quite moist. Then place the ravioli, spaced slightly apart, on a floured surface. Allow the dough sheets for ribbon or strand pasta to air-dry on a floured surface for about 15 minutes. To cut wide ribbon pasta such as pappardelle, see page 22. To cut strand pasta such as linguine, roll up the dough sheet, flatten the top slightly, and cut the roll crosswise into the desired width. If cutting strand pasta by machine, secure the desired cutting attachment and pass the sheet through the cutters. Put the strands on a floured work surface or baking sheet. Toss occasionally to prevent sticking.

Ribbon and strand pastas can be stored if not cooked immediately. Loosely form them into small nests, dusting them with flour. Let rest for 30 minutes until leathery but not brittle, then wrap airtight and refrigerate for no more than 2 days.

ROLLING OUT, CUTTING, AND FILLING PASTA FOR RAVIOLI

Before rolling out pasta dough, be sure the pasta machine is securely attached to the work surface. For making ravioli, have ready the pasta dough (page 110); the filling (see Butternut Squash Ravioli, page 55); the egg wash (1 large egg beaten with 1 teaspoon water) for sealing the ravioli; a tablespoon measure for spooning the filling; and a straight-edged pastry cutter or sharp knife for cutting the filled ravioli.

If you are making ribbon or strand pasta or sheets for cannelloni, rather than ravioli, follow steps 1 and 2 only. For additional information on rolling out pasta dough, see page 110.

1 **Rolling out the dough:** Adjust the rollers to the widest setting, lightly dust the dough, and pass the dough through the rollers 8 to 10 times until it is smooth, folding it in half after each pass and dusting it very lightly with flour if it tears.

2 **Achieving the desired thinness:** Reset the rollers one width narrower and pass the dough through them. Repeat, passing the dough, without folding, and using a narrower setting each time, until the dough is the desired thinness. Dust with flour as needed.

3 **Spooning on the filling:** Place a sheet of pasta on a lightly floured work surface. Using a tablespoon, place spoonfuls of the filling on the sheet at 2-inch (5-cm) intervals. Lightly brush the exposed dough surface with the egg wash.

4 **Cutting the ravioli:** Carefully top with a second sheet of pasta. Using your fingers, press the area around each mound of filling to seal. Using a pastry wheel or sharp, thin knife, cut into 2-inch (5-cm) squares, then press the edges firmly to seal.

BASIC RECIPES

Here are some of the basic recipes referred to throughout this book.

PASTA DOUGH

3 cups (15 oz/470 g) unbleached all-purpose (plain) flour, plus more for kneading and rolling

4 large eggs

1 tablespoon safflower oil

To make the dough in a food processor, place the flour in the work bowl. In a measuring pitcher with a spout, whisk together the eggs and oil. With the machine running, slowly drizzle in the egg mixture through the feed tube until the dough starts to come away from the sides of the bowl; you may not need all of the liquid. Process for 30 seconds longer, and check the consistency by pinching a bit of dough. It should be moist enough to hold together, but not sticky. If it is not, process a few seconds longer and test again.

To make the dough by hand, place the flour in a mound on a wooden or plastic work surface. Make a well in the center. In a measuring pitcher with a spout, whisk together the eggs and oil. Pour the egg mixture into the well. Then, using your fingers and working in a circular motion, gradually blend the egg mixture into the flour.

Lightly flour your hands, gather the dough into a ball, and knead, adding additional flour in small amounts as needed to prevent stickiness, until smooth and elastic, 10–15 minutes.

Place the dough in a plastic bag and let it rest at room temperature for 30 minutes to relax the dough before rolling.

Cut the dough into 4 equal pieces and return 3 pieces to the bag to prevent them from drying out.

To roll out the dough on a pasta machine, adjust the rollers to the widest setting. Flatten the piece of dough with your hand, lightly dust it with flour, and pass the dough through the rollers. Fold the dough in half and pass it through the rollers a second time. Repeat the rolling and folding 6–8 more times, or until the dough is smooth. Flour the dough lightly if it tears or starts to stick, brushing off the excess flour. Reset the rollers one width narrower and pass the dough through them. Again reset one width narrower and repeat, passing the dough, without folding, through the rollers. Continue to put the dough through the rollers, without folding it and using a narrower setting for each pass, until the sheet of dough is the desired thinness, usually the second to last setting for ribbon pasta and the last setting for stuffed pasta such as ravioli or cannelloni. Each sheet will be 4–5 inches (10–13 cm) wide. For more information on rolling out pasta dough, see page 106.

To roll out the dough by hand, dust the work surface with flour, place a dough portion on it, and flatten the dough with your palm. Then, using light pressure—you want to stretch the dough gently, not press it hard—roll it out evenly into a round. Always roll away from you and regularly rotate the disk a quarter turn as it becomes thinner and thinner. The dough is sufficiently thin if your hand is visible through it when it is held up to the light.

For ribbon pasta such as pappardelle (page 22) or for strand pasta, lay the finished sheets out on a lightly floured surface and let rest for 15 minutes before cutting. For filled pasta, cut the sheets as directed in individual recipes for ravioli (pages 48 and 55) or cannelloni (page 56). If you are not using the sheets immediately for filled pasta, keep in a plastic bag until using. Makes about 1 lb (500 g) pasta dough.

CROSTINI

1 baguette or 1 loaf coarse country bread

Extra-virgin olive oil for brushing (optional)

Preheat the oven to 350°F (180°C).

If using a baguette, cut on the diagonal into 18 slices ½ inch (12 mm) thick. If using coarse country bread, cut into ½-inch-thick slices, cutting the slices in half on the diagonal if they are large.

Arrange the bread slices on a baking sheet and brush them lightly with olive oil, if desired. Bake until golden, 10–15 minutes. Remove from the oven and serve. Makes 18 *crostini.*

Serving Tip: Top the crostini *with savory spreads (page 28) and serve as a starter, or offer the* crostini *as an accompaniment to soups or salads.*

COOKING PASTA

Cooking pasta requires a generous amount of water to prevent sticking, so you will need a good-sized pot. Some cooks prefer a large pot with a strainer insert, which eliminates the need for a colander for draining.

Use at least 6 quarts (6 l) cold water for each pound (500 g) of pasta you are cooking—the pot should be no more than three-fourths full—and bring to a rolling boil over high heat. Liberally salt the water, using at least 1 tablespoon salt for each pound of pasta. When the water returns to the boil, quickly add the pasta all at once while stirring constantly. When all the pasta is in the pot and the water returns to the boil, adjust the heat to maintain a steady, but not hard, boil. Cook uncovered, stirring frequently to prevent sticking.

Fresh pasta cooks quickly. Pappardelle and ravioli will be ready in 2–3 minutes, while finer strands may take no more than 1 minute. Dried pasta, which must rehydrate, takes longer, typically 7–8 minutes for spaghetti and other long, thin cuts and 8–10 minutes for short, stocky cuts. All pasta should have some firmness at the center when it is ready, a quality the Italians call *al dente,* "to the tooth." To test, bite into a sample and look at the cross-section. The outer part cooks first and its color will have darkened. The uncooked part in the center will still be white. When that white is about to disappear, the pasta is done.

The ambient heat will continue to cook the pasta, and it will be at the perfect consistency by the time it reaches the table. If you test the pasta and you fear that you might have overcooked it, try saving it by immediately adding cold water to the pot to stop the cooking.

BUYING PASTA

Dried pasta, whether spaghetti, fusilli, or bucatini, calls for only flour and water. Yet how these two ingredients are handled determines the taste and the nutritional value of the finished pasta. Look for first-rate factory-made and artisanal pastas imported from Italy. The best products are made from durum (hard) wheat; are extruded through bronze dies, which guarantee a texture that will hold a sauce; and undergo a long, cool-air drying process, which preserves nutrients.

Fresh pasta sheets are now sold in some markets and in specialty-food stores. Those made with egg ensure a more tender texture but also mean a shorter shelf life, so use them soon after purchase.

MAKING RISOTTO

Italy grows a number of rice varieties for different uses. Among them are large-grained, high-starch Arborio and Carnaroli, two excellent choices for making risotto, a northern Italian specialty in which rice is slowly simmered and stirred in hot liquid until the kernels are tender and moist but still chewy at the center. Arborio, a popular export, is the better known of the two varieties outside Italy, but Carnaroli makes a superior risotto because of its extremely high starch content.

For the best risotto, look for imported Italian rice packed in canvas bags that allow the kernels to breathe, checking the sell-by date before purchase. While vacuum packing and other airtight packaging keeps out insects, they also deprive the grains of air, which reduces the amount of liquid they can absorb once they are on the stove. The kernels should be opaque and have a uniform color and smooth surface. You will know you have purchased old or improperly stored rice if you scoop some up and it leave traces of starchy powder on your hand or if it has an off odor. Store rice in a cool, well-ventilated cupboard.

Plan on 3 cups (21 oz/655 g) raw rice for 6 servings for a first course.

The cooked rice will double in volume. Choose a wide, heavy-bottomed pot. The broad surface helps to distribute heat evenly and steadily, producing a uniform reduction of the liquid as the rice cooks, and the heavy base prevents scorching. Have all your ingredients at room temperature or heated. The addition of cold ingredients will shock the rice, causing it to stay hard at the core, and will slow down and inhibit the release of the starch in the grains that gives the dish its characteristic finish.

The making of risotto follows a few simple steps. Most recipes start with sautéing onion and/or garlic. Cook them only until they are softened; they should not brown. Sometimes the main flavoring ingredient, such as mushrooms, is also added at this point, nearly fully cooked, removed and set aside while the rice simmers, and then returned to the pan at the end to heat through. Cooking these ingredients first releases some of their flavor into the pan, which is absorbed at once by the rice.

Next, add the rice and "lightly toast" it in the butter and/or oil for 3–4 minutes to coat the grains with the fat, a liquid-resistant shield that will inhibit overly rapid absorption of the cooking liquid. This step encourages an even release of the starch for a more consistent creaminess in the finished risotto. The rice should not brown but rather turn from opaque to translucent with a white dot visible at the center of each grain.

Now, pour in the wine and deglaze the pan, stirring to loosen any cooked bits stuck to the bottom. Then, as you begin to add the stock a ladleful at a time, stir frequently and adjust the temperature as needed. The rice should cook briskly, but not so fast that the grains begin to fall apart. Always keep the grains bathed in a little stock and stir frequently.

The total cooking time, from the moment the stock is first added, is usually 18–20 minutes, but this can vary depending on the kind of rice used, how it has been processed, and the recipe. When finished, the risotto should be lightly creamy and the grains should be tender but firm, fluffy, and separate. Taste a few kernels to determine the doneness. Rice, like pasta, cooks from the residual heat even after it is transferred to a serving dish or individual plates. It also continues to release starch and absorb existing liquid. To prevent the risotto from becoming dry, a little stock (about ¼ cup/2 fl oz/60 ml) is added just before removing the pan from the heat and bringing the risotto to the table.

MARINATING MEAT

Italian cooks often marinate meats to tenderize and flavor them. To be effective, a marinade must contain an acidic ingredient, such as wine (see Vitello Tonnato, page 40) or citrus juice (see Rabbit with Roasted Garlic, page 75). For the best results, use a drinking-quality wine or freshly squeezed juice.

Marinating is more effective for small cuts than large cuts, as the marinade penetrates only the surface, and piercing the meat to allow the marinade to reach the center may cause it to dry out during cooking. Select a nonaluminum vessel (glass, stainless steel, or plastic) to prevent any chemical reaction with the acid, which can cause an off flavor or color. The vessel should be of a size that ensures that the meat is easily bathed in the liquid. It is important to turn the meat occasionally so every part of the surface comes into contact with the marinade. Cover and refrigerate any meat that is marinated for longer than 1 hour, and bring it to room temperature before cooking.

Some meats are cooked in their marinade for all or part of the time. After the meat is done, it is removed from the pan, and the liquid remaining in the pan is used to make a sauce for serving with the meat (see Brasato al Barolo, page 72).

BASIC RECIPES

Here are some of the basic recipes referred to throughout this book.

PASTA DOUGH

3 cups (15 oz/470 g) unbleached all-purpose (plain) flour, plus more for kneading and rolling

4 large eggs

1 tablespoon safflower oil

To make the dough in a food processor, place the flour in the work bowl. In a measuring pitcher with a spout, whisk together the eggs and oil. With the machine running, slowly drizzle in the egg mixture through the feed tube until the dough starts to come away from the sides of the bowl; you may not need all of the liquid. Process for 30 seconds longer, and check the consistency by pinching a bit of dough. It should be moist enough to hold together, but not sticky. If it is not, process a few seconds longer and test again.

To make the dough by hand, place the flour in a mound on a wooden or plastic work surface. Make a well in the center. In a measuring pitcher with a spout, whisk together the eggs and oil. Pour the egg mixture into the well. Then, using your fingers and working in a circular motion, gradually blend the egg mixture into the flour.

Lightly flour your hands, gather the dough into a ball, and knead, adding additional flour in small amounts as needed to prevent stickiness, until smooth and elastic, 10–15 minutes.

Place the dough in a plastic bag and let it rest at room temperature for 30 minutes to relax the dough before rolling.

Cut the dough into 4 equal pieces and return 3 pieces to the bag to prevent them from drying out.

To roll out the dough on a pasta machine, adjust the rollers to the widest setting. Flatten the piece of dough with your hand, lightly dust it with flour, and pass the dough through the rollers. Fold the dough in half and pass it through the rollers a second time. Repeat the rolling and folding 6–8 more times, or until the dough is smooth. Flour the dough lightly if it tears or starts to stick, brushing off the excess flour. Reset the rollers one width narrower and pass the dough through them. Again reset one width narrower and repeat, passing the dough, without folding, through the rollers. Continue to put the dough through the rollers, without folding it and using a narrower setting for each pass, until the sheet of dough is the desired thinness, usually the second to last setting for ribbon pasta and the last setting for stuffed pasta such as ravioli or cannelloni. Each sheet will be 4–5 inches (10–13 cm) wide. For more information on rolling out pasta dough, see page 106.

To roll out the dough by hand, dust the work surface with flour, place a dough portion on it, and flatten the dough with your palm. Then, using light pressure—you want to stretch the dough gently, not press it hard— roll it out evenly into a round. Always roll away from you and regularly rotate the disk a quarter turn as it becomes thinner and thinner. The dough is sufficiently thin if your hand is visible through it when it is held up to the light.

For ribbon pasta such as pappardelle (page 22) or for strand pasta, lay the finished sheets out on a lightly floured surface and let rest for 15 minutes before cutting. For filled pasta, cut the sheets as directed in individual recipes for ravioli (pages 48 and 55) or cannelloni (page 56). If you are not using the sheets immediately for filled pasta, keep in a plastic bag until using. Makes about 1 lb (500 g) pasta dough.

CROSTINI

1 baguette or 1 loaf coarse country bread

Extra-virgin olive oil for brushing (optional)

Preheat the oven to 350°F (180°C).

If using a baguette, cut on the diagonal into 18 slices ½ inch (12 mm) thick. If using coarse country bread, cut into ½-inch-thick slices, cutting the slices in half on the diagonal if they are large.

Arrange the bread slices on a baking sheet and brush them lightly with olive oil, if desired. Bake until golden, 10–15 minutes. Remove from the oven and serve. Makes 18 *crostini.*

Serving Tip: Top the crostini *with savory spreads (page 28) and serve as a starter, or offer the* crostini *as an accompaniment to soups or salads.*

CHICKEN STOCK

1 chicken, about 3 lb (1.5 kg), cut up, or 6 lb (3 kg) chicken parts such as backs, wings, and necks

1 carrot, peeled and cut into ½-inch (12-mm) pieces

1 celery stalk, cut into ½-inch (12-mm) pieces

1 yellow onion, cut into ½-inch (12-mm) pieces

1 bouquet garni (page 113)

In a stockpot, combine the chicken, carrot, celery, onion, bouquet garni, and 4 qt (4 l) water and bring to a boil over high heat. Reduce the heat to low and skim the foam from the top. Simmer, uncovered, for 2 hours, skimming occasionally.

Strain the stock through a sieve into another container and discard the solids. Let cool. Cover and refrigerate until the fat solidifies. Remove and discard the congealed fat. Cover and refrigerate for up to 3 days or freeze up to 3 months. Makes about 3 qt (3 l).

MEAT STOCK

6 lb (3 kg) beef or veal shank bones, cut into 3-inch (7.5-cm) lengths

2 yellow onions, cut into 1-inch (2.5-cm) pieces

2 carrots, peeled and cut into 1-inch (2.5-cm) pieces

1 celery stalk, cut into 1-inch (2.5-cm) pieces

1 bouquet garni (page 113)

Preheat the oven to 425°F (220°C). Put the bones and onions in a lightly oiled roasting pan and roast until well browned, 35–40 minutes. In a large stockpot, combine the bones, onions, carrots, celery, bouquet garni, and 12 qt (12 l) water and bring to a boil over high heat. Reduce the heat to low and skim the foam from the top. Simmer, uncovered, for at least 3 hours or up to 6 hours, skimming occasionally.

Strain the stock through a sieve into another container and discard the solids. Let cool. Cover and refrigerate until the fat solidifies. Remove and discard the congealed fat. Cover and refrigerate for up to 3 days or freeze up to 3 months. Makes about 5 qt (5 l).

VEGETABLE STOCK

¼ cup (2 fl oz/60 ml) extra-virgin olive oil

1 yellow onion, coarsely chopped

1 carrot, peeled and coarsely chopped

2 celery stalks, coarsely chopped

½ cup (4 fl oz/125 ml) dry white wine

1 bouquet garni (page 113)

In a stockpot, heat the olive oil over medium heat. Add the onion, carrot, and celery and sauté until lightly browned, 5–8 minutes. Add the wine and deglaze the pot, stirring to scrape up the browned bits from the bottom. Raise the heat to medium-high and cook until the wine is almost completely evaporated. Add 4 qt (4 l) water and the bouquet garni and bring to a boil. Reduce the heat to low and simmer, uncovered, for 45 minutes.

Strain the stock through a sieve into another container and discard the solids. Let cool completely. Cover and refrigerate for up to 3 days or freeze up to 3 months. Makes about 3½ qt (3.5 l).

GLOSSARY

AL DENTE Literally meaning "to the tooth," this Italian phrase refers to pasta or rice that has been cooked until tender but is still firm at the center, thus offering some resistance to the bite.

ARUGULA Also known as rocket, these slender green, deeply notched leaves have an appealing mild pepper taste and, especially when young, a tender texture.

BALSAMIC VINEGAR *Aceto balsamico tradizionale,* or traditional balsamic vinegar, comes from the Italian region of Emilia-Romagna. It is made from cooked grapes aged for varying periods in barrels constructed of a variety of aromatic woods. The final product is slightly thick and syrupy, with a sweet, mellow taste, and is used sparingly as a condiment on finished dishes. It should never be cooked. Balsamic vinegar of Modena, a town in Emilia-Romagna, is a younger wine vinegar flavored with caramel coloring and flavoring. Available widely outside Italy, it is added to vinaigrettes and used to make glazes for meat and in a preparation called *agrodolce* (page 31).

BEANS
Borlotti: Mottled beans with maroon speckles against a pink-beige background. Similar in appearance and flavor to cranberry beans, dried borlotti are used in soups, including the classic dish *pasta e fagioli* (page 13).

Cannellini: Ivory-colored beans possessing a fluffy texture when cooked. One of the most popular varieties in Italy, these dried beans are an ingredient in the soup called *ribollita* (page 18), are made into a purée for spreading on *crostini* (page 28), and are served as a side dish to accompany main courses. White kidney beans or Great Northern beans may be substituted if dried or canned cannellini beans are unavailable.

Cranberry: Similar to borlotti beans, cranberry beans are cream colored with red speckles. They can be used in any recipe that calls for borlotti beans.

BOUQUET GARNI A bouquet garni is a bundle of herbs and spices added at the start of cooking to flavor a stock, soup, or marinade. To make a bouquet garni for any of the stock recipes on page 111, place 4 fresh flat-leaf (Italian) parsley sprigs, 1 fresh thyme sprig, 1 bay leaf, and 4 or 5 peppercorns on a square of cheesecloth (muslin). Bring the corners together and tie securely with kitchen string to form a bundle. Retrieve and discard the bundle at the end of cooking. Follow the same procedure in other recipes that use herbs and spices as a bouquet garni.

BREAD CRUMBS, FRESH Crumbs, fresh as well as dried, are used to add body to pasta fillings and to coat meats and other ingredients before cooking.

To make bread crumbs, trim away the crusts from slices of day-old Italian- or French-style bread. Tear the bread into large pieces, put in a food processor, and process to the desired consistency.

CHEESE
Fontina: A cow's milk cheese with a mild and slightly nutty flavor, a firm and creamy texture, and a light but heady aroma. The Val d'Aosta, or Aosta Valley, of northwestern Italy produces the finest fontina, which is exported to markets outside the country.

Gorgonzola: A blue-veined cow's milk cheese from northern Italy with a moist, creamy texture and a complex flavor. It may be labeled *dolce* or *naturale.* The former is a young, mild cheese; the latter is aged, stronger tasting, and more aromatic. Dolcelatte, a particular brand of Gorgonzola *dolce,* is milder than other standard Gorgonzola cheeses.

Parmesan: A firm, aged, salty cheese made from cow's milk. Parmesan produced in the Emilia-Romagna region of Italy is known by the trademarked name Parmigiano-Reggiano. It has a rich, complex flavor and a pleasant granular texture that make it ideal for grating and sprinkling over pasta, stirring into risotto, adding to pesto, and using in ravioli fillings. To ensure freshness, purchase the cheese in wedges and grate or shave it only as needed for use in a recipe.

If true Parmigiano-Reggiano is not available, cheeses labeled "grana," a generic term for fine-grained hard grating cheeses made in the same area, may be substituted.

Whole-Milk Ricotta: To make cheese, rennet, a curdling agent, is added to milk, causing the solids to curdle. The curds are then drained, shaped, and aged. The liquid that remains after draining is the whey, which is processed further, or "recooked" (*ricotta* in Italian), to create ricotta cheese. Whole-milk ricotta is preferred for the recipes in this book, since skim-milk cheese tends to be more watery.

EGG, UNCOOKED Eggs that are used raw in a recipe or cooked to a temperature lower than 160°F (71°C) run a risk of being infected with salmonella or other types of bacteria, which can lead to food poisoning. This risk is of greatest concern to small children, pregnant women, older people, and anyone with a compromised immune system. If you have health concerns, do not consume raw egg, or seek out a pasteurized egg product to replace it. Note that the eggs in Spaghetti alla Carbonara (page 51) and Tiramisù (page 100), as well as coddled, poached, and boiled eggs, do not reach this temperature safety zone.

EGGPLANTS In Italian kitchens, eggplants (aubergines) are grilled; are rolled, stuffed with a filling, and then baked; and are also used in pasta sauces and classic dishes such as eggplant parmigiana and *caponata*. Most cooks are familiar with the globe eggplant, a variety that is usually large, resembles a pear in shape, and has a thin, shiny, deep purple skin. The produce sections of many markets also carry long, narrow Italian eggplants, which are smaller than globe eggplants and have deep purple skin. Yet other types have white, rose, green, or variegated skin. The color of the skin does not affect the flavor.

JUNIPER BERRIES These attractive blue-black berries, the size of small peas, are harvested from the evergreen juniper bush. They are added to marinades used to flavor assertive-tasting meats such as rabbit, lamb, and venison. Their best-known use is to flavor gin.

MARSALA Named for the Sicilian city in the area where it is made, Marsala is a fortified wine—that is, a wine preserved by the addition of brandy to raise the alcohol content. The rich-tasting, amber-colored wine is available in sweet and dry forms and is used in both savory and sweet dishes. Dry Marsala is enjoyed as an aperitif; sweet Marsala is a main ingredient in zabaglione (page 97) and is also enjoyed as a dessert wine.

MUSHROOMS

Chanterelle: Trumpet-shaped mushroom that is a bright golden yellow and has a flavor with hints of apricot. This variety grows in the wild and is not cultivated.

Oyster: A cream or pale gray mushroom that has a subtle shellfish taste. The caps fan out attractively from the stems. Oyster mushrooms are cultivated and grow in the wild.

Porcino: Classic Italian mushroom, with a rich, earthy flavor. Outside Italy, dried porcini are more readily available than fresh specimens. For more information, see page 17.

Portobello: A mature cremini mushroom that, at its largest, grows to 6 inches (15 cm) in diameter. Portobellos are dark brown and have a rich, meaty texture.

Shiitake: Dark brown or pale brown mushroom with tan undersides, a meaty texture, and a rich mushroom flavor.

OLIVE OIL Italy and other countries in the Mediterranean region produce excellent olive oils. Processing young green olives results in green oils such as those found in Tuscany. The oil from mature olives, like that from southern Italy, is more golden and buttery.

The highest grade of olive oil is labeled "extra-virgin," which refers to oil extracted from the fruit without the use of heat or chemicals. The quality of extra-virgin oils varies, but at its best the oil has a clear, greenish hue and a flavor that is fine, fruity, and sometimes slightly peppery.

PANCETTA See page 51.

PASTA SHAPES

Bucatini: Long, narrow tubes resembling hollow spaghetti.

Fusilli: Spirals that are twisted like corkscrews or "springs." The many curves are ideal for holding chunky or thick, creamy sauces.

Linguine: "Little tongues." Flat, narrow ribbons of the same general length as spaghetti, about ⅛ inch (3 mm) wide.

Orecchiette: Small, concave "little ears."

Pappardelle: Ribbons of pasta that range from ½ inch (12 mm) to 1 inch (2.5 cm) in width (see page 22).

Spaghetti: Long, thin, cylindrical strands. The name derives from the Italian word for "strings."

PASTRY WHEEL Used to cut or trim pastry dough, a pastry wheel is practical for cutting pasta. The wheel is a circular straight or fluted blade attached to a handle that allows the wheel to be rolled across the dough.

PIZZA PEEL Cooks, especially professional bakers, place garnished pizzas on this wooden tool so they can be transferred to the oven safely and with ease. Peels measure 24 inches (60 cm) or more in diameter and have a thin edge and long handle. A rimless baking sheet can be used for the same purpose.

PIZZA STONE Also called a baking stone or baking tile, this square, rectangular, or round slab of unglazed stoneware creates the effect of a brick oven in a home oven. The stone should be preheated in the oven for at least 45 minutes or up to 1 hour before baking. The pizza or other bread is slid onto the hot stone from a pizza peel.

SAFFRON The stigmas of a type of crocus, saffron is used in many regions of Italy to add a subtle flavor and appealing yellow color to many dishes, including risottos, soups, and stews. For the best flavor, buy saffron in whole "threads," or stigmas, and check the date on the package to make sure the saffron has not been on the shelf too long.

SEMOLINA FLOUR This somewhat coarse flour is milled from durum wheat, a variety that is high in protein. The flour is preferred for use in the manufacture of dried pasta. It is also used in some pizza doughs and breads.

SHRIMP, DEVEINING Running through most shrimp is a dark intestinal vein that is usually removed before the shellfish are used in a recipe. The easiest method is to use a paring knife to make a shallow cut following the curve of the shrimp's back just deep enough to reach the vein. Slip the tip of the knife under the vein, pull it out, rinse the shrimp under cold water, and then pat dry.

SQUID Known in Italy as calamari, squid is a type of shellfish that has mild, sweet flesh. Because squid tends to become tough when overheated, it is generally cooked briefly in such dishes as Fritto Misto (page 36), Insalata Frutti di Mare (page 32), and pasta sauces.

Squid is often sold already cleaned. If you purchase whole squid and need to clean it yourself, begin by pulling the head and tentacles from the body pouch.

Discard the innards that are clinging to the head. Cut off the tentacles just below the eyes, and discard the eye portion. Squeeze the cut end of the tentacles to expel the hard, round beak, then discard it. Pull out and discard the long, transparent quill inside the body pouch. Rinse the body and tentacles under running cold water and peel the gray membrane from the body, using a paring knife to scrape off any clinging bits. The body can be cut crosswise into rings, and the tentacles can be cut into bite-sized pieces.

TOMATOES
Plum: Small tomato with a plump pear shape. Also called Roma or egg tomato, this variety of fresh tomato offers the best quality year-round. Plum tomatoes are also available canned.

San Marzano: Variety of plum tomato from southern Italy and considered the finest of its type. The tomatoes are canned and exported to markets outside the country.

Sun-Dried: Tomatoes that have been dried in the sun, a special dehydrator, or a low oven to intensify their flavor and make their texture dense and chewy. The tomatoes are preserved in olive oil or packaged dry. Those packed in oil are pliable and ready to add to cooked dishes; they also have more flavor than dry-packed tomatoes. The latter must be rehydrated in hot water for 30 minutes before using.

VIN SANTO See page 60.

INDEX

SIMON & SCHUSTER SOURCE
A Division of Simon & Schuster, Inc.
Rockefeller Center
1230 Avenue of the Americas
New York, NY 10020

WILLIAMS-SONOMA
Founder and Vice-Chairman: Chuck Williams

WELDON OWEN INC.
Chief Executive Officer: John Owen
President: Terry Newell
Chief Operating Officer: Larry Partington
Vice President, International Sales: Stuart Laurence
Creative Director: Gaye Allen
Series Editor: Sarah Putman Clegg
Managing Editor: Judith Dunham
Editor: Heather Belt
Designer: Teri Gardiner
Production Director: Chris Hemesath
Color Manager: Teri Bell
Shipping and Production Coordinator: Libby Temple

Weldon Owen wishes to thank the following
people for their generous assistance and support
in producing this book: Copy Editors Carolyn Miller and
Sharon Silva; Consulting Editor Carrie Bradley; Food Stylist
Sandra Cook; Assistant Food Stylists Elisabet
der Nederlanden, Melinda Barsales, and Annie Salisbury;
Recipe Consultant Peggy Fallon; Photographer's Assistants
Noriko Akiyama and Heidi Ladendorf; Proofreaders
Desne Ahlers and Carrie Bradley; Production Designer
Linda Bouchard; and Indexer Ken DellaPenta.

Set in Trajan, Utopia, and Vectora.

Williams-Sonoma Collection *Italian* was
conceived and produced by Weldon Owen Inc.,
814 Montgomery Street, San Francisco,
California 94133, in collaboration with
Williams-Sonoma, 3250 Van Ness Avenue,
San Francisco, California 94109.

A Weldon Owen Production
Copyright © 2003 by Weldon Owen Inc. and
Williams-Sonoma Inc.

For information regarding special discounts for
bulk purchases, please contact Simon & Schuster
Special Sales at 1-800-456-6798 or
business@simonandschuster.com

Color separations by Bright Arts Graphics
Singapore (Pte.) Ltd.
Printed and bound in Singapore by Tien Wah
Press (Pte.) Ltd.

First printed in 2003.

10 9 8 7 6 5 4 3 2

Library of Congress Cataloging-in-Publication
data is available.

ISBN 0-7432-4995-X

A NOTE ON WEIGHTS AND MEASURES

All recipes include customary U.S. and metric measurements. Metric conversions are based on
a standard developed for this book and have been rounded off. Actual weights may vary.